The Believer's Journal for Everyday Faith

By Kerry Evelyn

ORANGE BLOSSOM
PUBLISHING

Maitland, Florida

DEDICATION

To the Lifesong moms, who breathed life into my faith when it was dying, and to all my "stretcher bearers," who carry me when I can't walk on my own

© 2021 Kerry Evelyn
All rights reserved. No part of this book may be transmitted in any form or by any means, electronic or mechanical, including photocopying, recording, or by any information storage or retrieval system, in part, in any form, without the permission of the publisher.

Published 2021 by Orange Blossom Publishing
Maitland, Florida
www.orangeblossombooks.com
info@orangeblossombooks.com

ISBN: 978-1-949935-28-8

THIS JOURNAL BELONGS TO

....

Note: All versus quoted from the New International Version of the Bible. Also, there are **additional pages in the back** of the book for more space with monthly reflections

A Note from Kerry

When I was growing up, there was more of an emphasis on recitation prayer and teaching, but not as much on creating a personal relationship with Christ. A relationship with Jesus may sound strange to you. Think of it as a mindset shift, or a lens with which to view and process all the things.

As I got older, I felt a longing for something more. In my late teens and early twenties, I stopped going to church regularly. It was the same message over and over again. It wasn't enough for me, and I started researching Bible history. I wanted to know more about the men and women who made such an impact on the world, the mistakes they made, the grace they gave, and their journeys of faith. Ultimately, God gave us two rules: love Him, and love your neighbor as yourself. I knew I was overcomplicating His Word, and I longed for someone to help me make sense of it all.

In 2009, I was expecting my second child, and my neighbor encouraged me to put my then two-year-old daughter in a preschool program at our neighborhood church. One Friday a month the moms got together as a Mothers of Preschoolers group (MOPs) and she dragged me to that as well. It was a turning point for me. I met some wonderful friends in that group and joined the women's Bible study. For the first time in my life, I felt connected to Jesus. Up until then, He seemed like the superhero that was perfect, and I could never hope to be.

I learned a ton. I prayed out loud for the first time in my life, and it wasn't a recitation. I held hands with women who thanked God for food before eating, and it wasn't even Thanksgiving, Christmas, or Easter! So, six years later, I was primed and ready for what to hear the message that would ultimately lead me to write my first book. And when that second book started coming out, which was the first book I published, it was very different from what I had imagined.

I learned how to use the Bible as a workbook from a trusted mentor, who also challenged me to write my first book. I started out writing a historical World War II saga and ended up with a contemporary Christian romance. I don't know how that happened. The only explanation was that God gave me the words. I didn't even realize until my characters struggled and used their faith to help them that I was doing the same thing in my life. It just came natural to me. But it took me years to get to that point, and even longer to figure out that was what happened.

God always shows up. He lives in you. You just have to give yourself permission to listen to Him and feel Him. And if you're on the path He's laid out for you, you'll see Him more. I knew when I was a kid I wanted to move to Florida. I didn't know how or when I would get here, but it wasn't just a dream for me. I knew at some point I would make it happen. I believed in God's timing. And I believe that when you are not on the right path, sometimes He sends you a redirection. I graduated college, and my first two years of teaching were quite the struggle bus! After September 11th, 2001, I was laid off, along with hundreds of other people who had three years or less in the school department I taught for. I made a joke to my friend who is from Orlando, asking if her sister needed a roommate because I was either done with teaching or relocating far away. She said no, but her brother had just purchased a house and was looking for a third roommate. I applied to some schools in the Orlando area, and the school that was meant for me called me back.

After speaking on the phone for a little over an hour, the principal wanted to hire me on the spot without having met me in person.

If that wasn't a sign from God that I was supposed to be in Florida, I don't know what was. So that July I moved down, and within a couple of weeks, I met the man who would become my husband. I needed that push to be laid off in order to make the move. I don't know if I would have done it on my own.

Another time I let God lead was when I decided to homeschool my children. As an elementary school teacher, the idea both shocked and terrified me. Sure, I could teach a classroom full of kids, but my own? Every day? Year after year? I didn't know how I was going to do it, but God showed up, and opened doors to an entire community and a hybrid homeschool/private school option that we've now been a part of going on ten years.

When my children displayed learning differences in kindergarten, I watched them carefully. By second grade, it was evident we had two highly intelligent students whose gifts and talents and struggles would benefit from personalized curriculum and instruction. I was overwhelmed with gratitude that we had a community of support, and I still thank God every day for leading me to trust Him and not settle for the status quo. I've always been one to take the road less traveled over what's easy and logical. I reinvent wheels all the time. He made me this way, and I've learned to embrace it because I know my experiences will benefit others.

People often tell me they think I was brave to move down here by myself, that I'm brave to homeschool my children, but I wasn't ever by myself. God was with me; He is with me, and He has given me a support network until I could make it on my own. It's been nineteen years in Florida, nine+ years homeschooling, and I know I'm where I'm supposed to be and what I'm supposed to be doing. Other struggles have popped up, like independent publishing (talk about the road less traveled!) and I've sought God's guidance for all of them. With Him, anything is possible.

How to Use this Book

Select a Focus Word for the Year
Choose a word to use as a filter/lens for which you take in/process the rest of this book, no matter where you start. For example, my focus word for the year is *refine*. If I'm starting this journal in April, I will use *refine* as my guiding word until December 31, and then my new word will take over. You may also choose to use the same word for the duration of the journal, no matter how many years it spans. Unsure what to do? Pray about it, then go with your gut. It's likely God offering His input.
(See the activity in a few pages to select your word.)

Adjust Your View: God's Role in your Life
The bigger you make your problems, the smaller He becomes. The reverse is also true, and a crucial concept for applying faith to everyday life. Similar to the wave of love you feel when you're overwhelmed with happy news, one must view the world through a lens of God's love to see and experience the peace and joy that comes from secure faith in Him.

Each Month
This journal is divided into twelve four-week sections, with a new topic each month. Whether you start January first or midway through the year, be sure to follow in order without skipping. The content is designed to build on previous skills and heartwork you'll do along the way. Without defining your vision in Month 1, you won't know how to best focus your finances in Month 10.

Each Week
Start your week with the Focus Verse. Write it out, and reflect on it. Decide what you will focus on and write it down. For example, for Week 1, your focus may be to create a vision board or adapt a mindset to be at peace with something that you've struggled with.

Based on your focus, write a positive affirmation to meditate on and state out loud several times a day. If your focus was to be at peace with a past failing, your affirmation may sound like this: "I am focused on what's next. I will let the Lord lead me to my destiny."

Each Day
Set aside time in the morning and at night to pray, reflect, and record.

Each Quarter
Every three months, you'll reflect on what you've learned, how you've grown, and the work you still need to do. You'll record answered prayers, and refine your focus and vision.

Everyday Faith Inventory

Take a few moments to evaluate your current spiritual status.

Date: ....

	Always	Sometimes	Never
I purposefully set aside time daily to be with God			
I feel connected to God			
I can hear God			
I listen to God			
I give my day to God			
I have peace things will work out			
I am productive, but not busy			
I give myself grace			
I give others grace			
I am able to keep calm in stressful situations			
I am able to rest			
My body feels loose and light			
I can express gratitude where I am			
I am a peace with my past			
I can find joy in everywhere			
I am content and at rest			
My faith is unshakable			

Choose Your Focus Word

Choose One Word to Inform Your Focus
Don't spend too long thinking about this. Tune into your subconscious and write down the first ten words that come to mind. Then, pray over them and see which one becomes prevalent in your mind. That's likely the filter word you'll need while working through this journal.

....
....
....
....
....
....
....
....
....
....

My Focus Word:

Your Tasks

Remember God's Promise
Gen 28:15 I am with you and will watch over you wherever you go, and I will bring you back to this land. I will not leave you until I have done what I have promised you.

Keep the Faith
1 Thessalonians 5:16-18 Rejoice always, pray continually, and give thanks in all circumstances; for this is God's will for you in Christ Jesus.

Your Goals

Create a Vision

Jot down your goals and vision for the following twelve areas of your life. You must know your destination in order to inform your choices as you make your way to living the life you are meant to live. Ideally, what do you want to achieve in each area? (extra pages in back)

1) Vision for your life (now vs. ideal)
....
....

2) Your ideal day
....
....

3) Healthy mindset
....
....

4) Healthy body
....
....

5) Education
....
....

6) Family
....
....

7) Friendships

....

....

8) Professional

....

....

9) Service/Philanthropy

....

....

10) Finances

....

....

11) Margin (unscheduled time)

....

....

12) Finding unshakable peace and joy where you're at

....

....

Work Toward Making that Vision Materialize

Use this journal as a guide to articulating and refining your goals, and always let God inform your decisions. Pray, seek His guidance, and listen for His voice as you navigate the journey of strengthening your everyday faith.

Month One: A Vision for Your Life

Think back to when you were younger, and write a few sentences detailing how you pictured your life would be up to this point.

....
....
....
....
....
....

Now, take a moment to express gratitude for the life you are living now. What is great about it? Where does it fall short of the plans you had? (extra pages in back)

....
....
....
....
....
....
....
....

Oftentimes, the plans we have are not the plans God has for us. When we aren't on the path that is meant for us, we will constantly be confronted with opposition. Some struggle is needed to climb and grow, but if that struggle doesn't feel right to you, you many have veered off your intended path. This month, we'll explore how to find the path, stay on it, and thrive on our journey down it.

Verses for the Month

Write these verses by hand at the beginning of each week. Then record any thoughts, feelings, or reflections that come to mind.

Week 1

Habakkuk 2:2-3 And the Lord answered me: "Write the vision; make it plain on tablets, so he may run who reads it." For still the vision awaits its appointed time; it hastens to the end—it will not lie. If it seems slow, wait for it; it will surely come; it will not delay.

………………………………………………………………………………………………
………………………………………………………………………………………………
………………………………………………………………………………………………
………………………………………………………………………………………………
………………………………………………………………………………………………
………………………………………………………………………………………………
………………………………………………………………………………………………
………………………………………………………………………………………………

Week 2

Jeremiah 29:11 For I know the plans I have for you, declares the Lord, plans for welfare and not for evil, to give you a future and a hope.

………………………………………………………………………………………………
………………………………………………………………………………………………
………………………………………………………………………………………………
………………………………………………………………………………………………
………………………………………………………………………………………………
………………………………………………………………………………………………
………………………………………………………………………………………………
………………………………………………………………………………………………

Week 3
Proverbs 19:21 Many are the plans in a person's heart, but it is the LORD's purpose that prevails.

....
....
....
....
....
....
....
....

Week 4
Psalm 46:5 God is within her; she will not fall; God will help her at break of day.

....
....
....
....
....
....
....
....

How do these verses apply to your focus word for this year?

....
....
....
....
....
....

Habakkuk 2:2-3 And the Lord answered me: "Write the vision; make it plain on tablets, so he may run who reads it." For still the vision awaits its appointed time; it hastens to the end—it will not lie. If it seems slow, wait for it; it will surely come; it will not delay.

My Focus This Week:
....
....
....
....

My Affirmation or Focus Statement:
....
....
....
....

Sunday: AM   PM

My prayer for today	Where I saw/heard God
What I'm giving to God	Successes
Distractions to be aware of	Challenges
I'm grateful for	Prayer requests

Monday: AM   PM

My prayer for today	Where I saw/heard God
What I'm giving to God	Successes
Distractions to be aware of	Challenges
I'm grateful for	Prayer requests

Tuesday: AM   PM

My prayer for today	Where I saw/heard God
What I'm giving to God	Successes
Distractions to be aware of	Challenges
I'm grateful for	Prayer requests

Wednesday: AM · PM

My prayer for today	Where I saw/heard God
What I'm giving to God	Successes
Distractions to be aware of	Challenges
I'm grateful for	Prayer requests

Thursday: AM · PM

My prayer for today	Where I saw/heard God
What I'm giving to God	Successes
Distractions to be aware of	Challenges
I'm grateful for	Prayer requests

Friday: AM   PM

My prayer for today	Where I saw/heard God
What I'm giving to God	Successes
Distractions to be aware of	Challenges
I'm grateful for	Prayer requests

Saturday: AM   PM

My prayer for today	Where I saw/heard God
What I'm giving to God	Successes
Distractions to be aware of	Challenges
I'm grateful for	Prayer requests

Jeremiah 29:11 For I know the plans I have for you, declares the Lord, plans for welfare and not for evil, to give you a future and a hope.

My Focus This Week:
....
....
....
....

My Affirmation or Focus Statement:
....
....
....
....

Sunday: AM   PM

My prayer for today	Where I saw/heard God
What I'm giving to God	Successes
Distractions to be aware of	Challenges
I'm grateful for	Prayer requests

Wednesday: AM   PM

My prayer for today	Where I saw/heard God
What I'm giving to God	Successes
Distractions to be aware of	Challenges
I'm grateful for	Prayer requests

Thursday: AM   PM

My prayer for today	Where I saw/heard God
What I'm giving to God	Successes
Distractions to be aware of	Challenges
I'm grateful for	Prayer requests

Friday: AM   PM

My prayer for today	Where I saw/heard God
What I'm giving to God	Successes
Distractions to be aware of	Challenges
I'm grateful for	Prayer requests

Saturday: AM   PM

My prayer for today	Where I saw/heard God
What I'm giving to God	Successes
Distractions to be aware of	Challenges
I'm grateful for	Prayer requests

Proverbs 19:21 Many are the plans in a person's heart, but it is the LORD's purpose that prevails.

My Focus This Week:
....
....
....
....

My Affirmation or Focus Statement:
....
....
....
....

Sunday: AM PM

My prayer for today	Where I saw/heard God
What I'm giving to God	Successes
Distractions to be aware of	Challenges
I'm grateful for	Prayer requests

Monday: AM   PM

My prayer for today	Where I saw/heard God
What I'm giving to God	Successes
Distractions to be aware of	Challenges
I'm grateful for	Prayer requests

Tuesday: AM   PM

My prayer for today	Where I saw/heard God
What I'm giving to God	Successes
Distractions to be aware of	Challenges
I'm grateful for	Prayer requests

Wednesday: AM   PM

My prayer for today	Where I saw/heard God
What I'm giving to God	Successes
Distractions to be aware of	Challenges
I'm grateful for	Prayer requests

Thursday: AM   PM

My prayer for today	Where I saw/heard God
What I'm giving to God	Successes
Distractions to be aware of	Challenges
I'm grateful for	Prayer requests

Friday: AM   PM

My prayer for today	Where I saw/heard God
What I'm giving to God	Successes
Distractions to be aware of	Challenges
I'm grateful for	Prayer requests

Saturday: AM   PM

My prayer for today	Where I saw/heard God
What I'm giving to God	Successes
Distractions to be aware of	Challenges
I'm grateful for	Prayer requests

Week Four

Psalm 46:5 God is within her; she will not fall; God will help her at break of day.

My Focus This Week:

....
....
....
....

My Affirmation or Focus Statement:

....
....
....
....

Sunday:

AM	PM
My prayer for today	Where I saw/heard God
What I'm giving to God	Successes
Distractions to be aware of	Challenges
I'm grateful for	Prayer requests

Monday:　　AM　　　　　　　　　　PM

My prayer for today	Where I saw/heard God
What I'm giving to God	Successes
Distractions to be aware of	Challenges
I'm grateful for	Prayer requests

Tuesday:　　AM　　　　　　　　　　PM

My prayer for today	Where I saw/heard God
What I'm giving to God	Successes
Distractions to be aware of	Challenges
I'm grateful for	Prayer requests

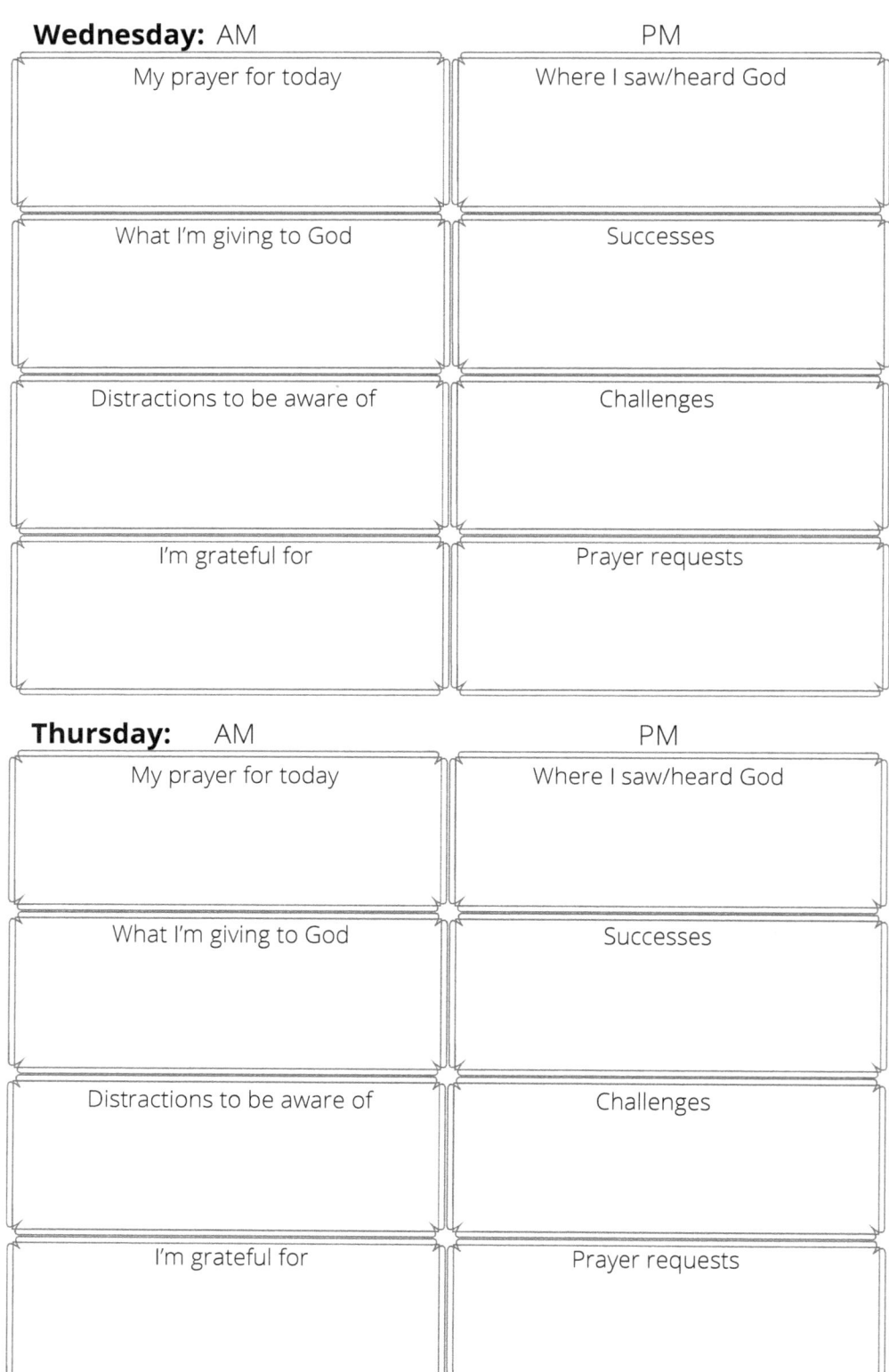

Friday: AM   PM

My prayer for today	Where I saw/heard God
What I'm giving to God	Successes
Distractions to be aware of	Challenges
I'm grateful for	Prayer requests

Saturday: AM   PM

My prayer for today	Where I saw/heard God
What I'm giving to God	Successes
Distractions to be aware of	Challenges
I'm grateful for	Prayer requests

Monthly Reflection

Use this space to reflect on your previous month.

....
....
....
....
....
....
....
....
....
....
....
....
....
....
....
....
....
....
....
....
....
....
....
....

Month Two: Daily Design

Take a moment to write out your typical week day and weekend day. (extra pages in back)

....
....
....
....
....
....

Are you running your day or is your day running you? I've found that when I design my day, it's intentional, productive, and I can roll with any punches that come at me. But if I wake up late and rush from task to task, it's a battle from the moment I get out of bed. I start the morning with a prayer and give time to God every day. When He leads my day, I'm more at peace with it.

Design your ideal weekday and weekend day(s). What steps can you take this month to transform your day from your current status quo?

....
....
....
....
....
....
....
....
....
....

Verses for the Month

Write these verses by hand at the beginning of each week. Then record any thoughts, feelings, or reflections that come to mind.

Week 1

Philippians 2:14 Do all things without murmurings and disputings.

....
....
....
....
....
....
....
....
....
....

Week 2

Proverbs 31:29 Many women do noble things, but you surpass them all.

....
....
....
....
....
....
....
....
....
....

Week 3

Colossians 3:12 Clothe yourself with compassion, kindness, humility, gentleness, and patience...

....
....
....
....
....
....
....
....
....

Week 4

Galatians 6:9 Let us not become weary in doing good, for at the proper time we will reap a harvest if we do not give up.

....
....
....
....
....
....
....
....

How do these verses apply to your focus word for this year?

....
....
....
....
....
....

Week One

Philippians 2:14 Do all things without murmurings and disputings.

My Focus This Week:
....
....
....
....

My Affirmation or Focus Statement:
....
....
....
....

Sunday:

AM	PM
My prayer for today	Where I saw/heard God
What I'm giving to God	Successes
Distractions to be aware of	Challenges
I'm grateful for	Prayer requests

Monday: AM   PM

My prayer for today	Where I saw/heard God
What I'm giving to God	Successes
Distractions to be aware of	Challenges
I'm grateful for	Prayer requests

Tuesday: AM   PM

My prayer for today	Where I saw/heard God
What I'm giving to God	Successes
Distractions to be aware of	Challenges
I'm grateful for	Prayer requests

Wednesday: AM   PM

My prayer for today	Where I saw/heard God
What I'm giving to God	Successes
Distractions to be aware of	Challenges
I'm grateful for	Prayer requests

Thursday: AM   PM

My prayer for today	Where I saw/heard God
What I'm giving to God	Successes
Distractions to be aware of	Challenges
I'm grateful for	Prayer requests

Proverbs 31:29 Many women do noble things, but you surpass them all.

My Focus This Week:

....
....
....
....

My Affirmation or Focus Statement:

....
....
....
....

Sunday: AM PM

My prayer for today	Where I saw/heard God
What I'm giving to God	Successes
Distractions to be aware of	Challenges
I'm grateful for	Prayer requests

Monday: AM　　　　　　　　　　PM

My prayer for today	Where I saw/heard God
What I'm giving to God	Successes
Distractions to be aware of	Challenges
I'm grateful for	Prayer requests

Tuesday: AM　　　　　　　　　　PM

My prayer for today	Where I saw/heard God
What I'm giving to God	Successes
Distractions to be aware of	Challenges
I'm grateful for	Prayer requests

Wednesday: AM   PM

My prayer for today	Where I saw/heard God
What I'm giving to God	**Successes**
Distractions to be aware of	**Challenges**
I'm grateful for	**Prayer requests**

Thursday: AM   PM

My prayer for today	Where I saw/heard God
What I'm giving to God	**Successes**
Distractions to be aware of	**Challenges**
I'm grateful for	**Prayer requests**

Friday: AM   PM

My prayer for today	Where I saw/heard God

What I'm giving to God	Successes

Distractions to be aware of	Challenges

I'm grateful for	Prayer requests

Saturday: AM   PM

My prayer for today	Where I saw/heard God

What I'm giving to God	Successes

Distractions to be aware of	Challenges

I'm grateful for	Prayer requests

Colossians 3:12 Clothe yourself with compassion, kindness, humility, gentleness, and patience...

My Focus This Week:
....
....
....
....

My Affirmation or Focus Statement:
....
....
....
....

Sunday:

AM	PM
My prayer for today	Where I saw/heard God
What I'm giving to God	Successes
Distractions to be aware of	Challenges
I'm grateful for	Prayer requests

Monday: AM PM

My prayer for today	Where I saw/heard God
What I'm giving to God	Successes
Distractions to be aware of	Challenges
I'm grateful for	Prayer requests

Tuesday: AM PM

My prayer for today	Where I saw/heard God
What I'm giving to God	Successes
Distractions to be aware of	Challenges
I'm grateful for	Prayer requests

Wednesday: AM   PM

My prayer for today	Where I saw/heard God
What I'm giving to God	Successes
Distractions to be aware of	Challenges
I'm grateful for	Prayer requests

Thursday: AM   PM

My prayer for today	Where I saw/heard God
What I'm giving to God	Successes
Distractions to be aware of	Challenges
I'm grateful for	Prayer requests

Friday: AM   PM

My prayer for today	Where I saw/heard God
What I'm giving to God	Successes
Distractions to be aware of	Challenges
I'm grateful for	Prayer requests

Saturday: AM   PM

My prayer for today	Where I saw/heard God
What I'm giving to God	Successes
Distractions to be aware of	Challenges
I'm grateful for	Prayer requests

Week Four

Galatians 6:9 Let us not become weary in doing good, for at the proper time we will reap a harvest if we do not give up.

My Focus This Week:

....
....
....
....

My Affirmation or Focus Statement:

....
....
....
....

Sunday:

AM	PM
My prayer for today	Where I saw/heard God
What I'm giving to God	Successes
Distractions to be aware of	Challenges
I'm grateful for	Prayer requests

Monday: AM　　　　　　　　　　　PM

My prayer for today	Where I saw/heard God

What I'm giving to God	Successes

Distractions to be aware of	Challenges

I'm grateful for	Prayer requests

Tuesday: AM　　　　　　　　　　PM

My prayer for today	Where I saw/heard God

What I'm giving to God	Successes

Distractions to be aware of	Challenges

I'm grateful for	Prayer requests

Wednesday: AM   PM

My prayer for today	Where I saw/heard God
What I'm giving to God	Successes
Distractions to be aware of	Challenges
I'm grateful for	Prayer requests

Thursday: AM   PM

My prayer for today	Where I saw/heard God
What I'm giving to God	Successes
Distractions to be aware of	Challenges
I'm grateful for	Prayer requests

Friday: AM   PM

My prayer for today	Where I saw/heard God
What I'm giving to God	Successes
Distractions to be aware of	Challenges
I'm grateful for	Prayer requests

Saturday: AM   PM

My prayer for today	Where I saw/heard God
What I'm giving to God	Successes
Distractions to be aware of	Challenges
I'm grateful for	Prayer requests

Monthly Reflection

Use this space to reflect on your previous month.

....
....
....
....
....
....
....
....
....
....
....
....
....
....
....
....
....
....
....
....
....
....

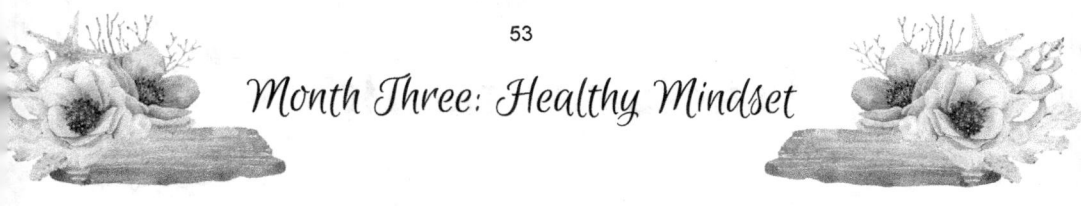

Month Three: Healthy Mindset

Romans 8:28 has been my guiding verse for decades. It brings me peace and reminds me that's it's okay to be okay with not understanding why things happen, and that my faith is what gives me peace.

The verses in this journal are prescriptive. They stand on their own to encourage, inspire, and remind us that God is there, waiting for us to seek Him. Reading His words and praying them out loud, especially, does a world of good, even if in hard times it doesn't seem helpful. Your brain is wired to defend itself, and along the same lines, it listens to your voice more than any other sound. You can truly re-program your brain! It takes time and effort, but it can be done.

When you believe God has plans for you and let Him lead you, He'll surprise you in ways you hadn't imagined. Sometimes we need to "let go and let God." Allow Him to work when you're struggling, and trust His timing. This month's verses will encourage you to trust Him, and yourself.

Write about the mindset you wish you had and what is holding you back. (extra pages in back)

....
....
....
....
....
....
....
....
....
....
....
....
....

Verses for the Month

Write these verses by hand at the beginning of each week. Then record any thoughts, feelings or reflections that come to mind.

Week 1

Romans 8:28 And we know that in all things God works for the good of those who love Him, who have been called according to His purpose.

....
....
....
....
....
....
....
....
....
....

Week 2

Romans 12:9 Love must be sincere. Hate what is evil; cling to what is good.

....
....
....
....
....
....
....
....
....
....

Week 3

Philipians 4:6-7 Do not be anxious about anything, but in every situation, by prayer and petition, with thanksgiving, present your requests to God. And the peace of God, which transcends all understanding, will guard your hearts and your minds in Christ Jesus.

....
....
....
....
....
....
....
....

Week 4

Psalm 5:3 In the morning, Lord, you hear my voice; in the morning I lay my requests before you and wait expectantly.

....
....
....
....
....
....
....
....

How do these verses apply to your focus word for this year?

....
....
....
....
....

Romans 8:28 And we know that in all things God works for the good of those who love Him, who have been called according to His purpose.

My Focus This Week:
....
....
....
....

My Affirmation or Focus Statement:
....
....
....
....

Sunday:

AM	PM
My prayer for today	Where I saw/heard God
What I'm giving to God	Successes
Distractions to be aware of	Challenges
I'm grateful for	Prayer requests

Wednesday: AM   PM

My prayer for today	Where I saw/heard God
What I'm giving to God	Successes
Distractions to be aware of	Challenges
I'm grateful for	Prayer requests

Thursday: AM   PM

My prayer for today	Where I saw/heard God
What I'm giving to God	Successes
Distractions to be aware of	Challenges
I'm grateful for	Prayer requests

Friday: AM   PM

My prayer for today	Where I saw/heard God
What I'm giving to God	Successes
Distractions to be aware of	Challenges
I'm grateful for	Prayer requests

Saturday: AM   PM

My prayer for today	Where I saw/heard God
What I'm giving to God	Successes
Distractions to be aware of	Challenges
I'm grateful for	Prayer requests

Romans 12:9 Love must be sincere. Hate what is evil; cling to what is good.

My Focus This Week:
....
....
....
....

My Affirmation or Focus Statement:
....
....
....
....

Sunday:

AM	PM
My prayer for today	Where I saw/heard God
What I'm giving to God	Successes
Distractions to be aware of	Challenges
I'm grateful for	Prayer requests

Monday: AM | PM

My prayer for today	Where I saw/heard God
What I'm giving to God	Successes
Distractions to be aware of	Challenges
I'm grateful for	Prayer requests

Tuesday: AM | PM

My prayer for today	Where I saw/heard God
What I'm giving to God	Successes
Distractions to be aware of	Challenges
I'm grateful for	Prayer requests

Wednesday: AM   PM

My prayer for today	Where I saw/heard God
What I'm giving to God	Successes
Distractions to be aware of	Challenges
I'm grateful for	Prayer requests

Thursday: AM   PM

My prayer for today	Where I saw/heard God
What I'm giving to God	Successes
Distractions to be aware of	Challenges
I'm grateful for	Prayer requests

Friday: AM → PM

My prayer for today	Where I saw/heard God
What I'm giving to God	Successes
Distractions to be aware of	Challenges
I'm grateful for	Prayer requests

Saturday: AM → PM

My prayer for today	Where I saw/heard God
What I'm giving to God	Successes
Distractions to be aware of	Challenges
I'm grateful for	Prayer requests

Week Three

Philippians 4:6-7 Do not be anxious about anything, but in every situation, by prayer and petition, with thanksgiving, present your requests to God. And the peace of God, which transcends all understanding, will guard your hearts and your minds in Christ Jesus.

My Focus This Week:
....
....
....
....

My Affirmation or Focus Statement:
....
....
....
....

Sunday:

AM	PM
My prayer for today	Where I saw/heard God
What I'm giving to God	Successes
Distractions to be aware of	Challenges
I'm grateful for	Prayer requests

Monday: AM   PM

My prayer for today	Where I saw/heard God
What I'm giving to God	Successes
Distractions to be aware of	Challenges
I'm grateful for	Prayer requests

Tuesday: AM   PM

My prayer for today	Where I saw/heard God
What I'm giving to God	Successes
Distractions to be aware of	Challenges
I'm grateful for	Prayer requests

Wednesday: AM   PM

My prayer for today	Where I saw/heard God
What I'm giving to God	Successes
Distractions to be aware of	Challenges
I'm grateful for	Prayer requests

Thursday: AM   PM

My prayer for today	Where I saw/heard God
What I'm giving to God	Successes
Distractions to be aware of	Challenges
I'm grateful for	Prayer requests

Friday: AM   PM

My prayer for today	Where I saw/heard God
What I'm giving to God	Successes
Distractions to be aware of	Challenges
I'm grateful for	Prayer requests

Saturday: AM   PM

My prayer for today	Where I saw/heard God
What I'm giving to God	Successes
Distractions to be aware of	Challenges
I'm grateful for	Prayer requests

Psalm 5:3 In the morning, Lord, you hear my voice; in the morning I lay my requests before you and wait expectantly.

My Focus This Week:
....
....
....
....

My Affirmation or Focus Statement:
....
....
....
....

Sunday:

AM	PM
My prayer for today	Where I saw/heard God
What I'm giving to God	Successes
Distractions to be aware of	Challenges
I'm grateful for	Prayer requests

Monday: AM PM

My prayer for today	Where I saw/heard God

What I'm giving to God	Successes

Distractions to be aware of	Challenges

I'm grateful for	Prayer requests

Tuesday: AM PM

My prayer for today	Where I saw/heard God

What I'm giving to God	Successes

Distractions to be aware of	Challenges

I'm grateful for	Prayer requests

Wednesday: AM   PM

My prayer for today	Where I saw/heard God
What I'm giving to God	Successes
Distractions to be aware of	Challenges
I'm grateful for	Prayer requests

Thursday: AM   PM

My prayer for today	Where I saw/heard God
What I'm giving to God	Successes
Distractions to be aware of	Challenges
I'm grateful for	Prayer requests

Friday: AM   PM

My prayer for today	Where I saw/heard God
What I'm giving to God	Successes
Distractions to be aware of	Challenges
I'm grateful for	Prayer requests

Saturday: AM   PM

My prayer for today	Where I saw/heard God
What I'm giving to God	Successes
Distractions to be aware of	Challenges
I'm grateful for	Prayer requests

Monthly Reflection

Use this space to reflect on your previous month.

....
....
....
....
....
....
....
....
....
....
....
....
....
....
....
....
....
....
....
....
....
....
....
....
....
....

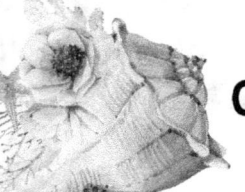

Quarterly Reflection

Proverbs 16:3 **Commit to the LORD whatever you do, and He will establish your plans.**

Have you committed your plans to the Lord? Do you have faith that He will see you through, even when your plans don't match up with His? Do you trust him to lead you where you're meant to go?

....
....
....
....
....
....
....
....
....
....
....
....
....
....
....
....
....
....
....
....
....
....
....
....

Answered Prayers

What prayers did God answer this quarter?

Month Four: Healthy Body

We have one body, and if we're not careful with it, it will fail us. We are designed perfectly for our purpose, and it's easy to lose that fact if we get caught up in worldly expectations and temptations.

Describe the body you have now. Does it look and feel the way you'd like it to? (extra pages in back)

....
....
....
....
....
....
....
....

Describe how you would like your body to look and feel.

....
....
....
....
....
....

What steps can you take to achieve the body you'd like to have?

....
....
....
....
....

Verses for the Month

Write these verses by hand at the beginning of each week. Then record any thoughts, feelings, or reflections that come to mind.

Week 1
Romans 8:28 And we know that in all things God works for the good of those who love Him, who have been called according to His purpose.

....
....
....
....
....
....
....
....
....

Week 2
Romans 12:9 Love must be sincere. Hate what is evil; cling to what is good.

....
....
....
....
....
....
....
....
....

Week 3

Philippians 4:6-7 Do not be anxious about anything, but in every situation, by prayer and petition, with thanksgiving, present your requests to God. And the peace of God, which transcends all understanding, will guard your hearts and your minds in Christ Jesus.

....
....
....
....
....
....
....
....

Week 4

Psalm 5:3 In the morning, LORD, you hear my voice; in the morning I lay my requests before you and wait expectantly.

....
....
....
....
....
....

How do these verses apply to your focus word for this year?

....
....
....
....
....

Romans 8:28 And we know that in all things God works for the good of those who love Him, who have been called according to His purpose.

My Focus This Week:
....
....
....
....

My Affirmation or Focus Statement:
....
....
....
....

Sunday:

AM	PM
My prayer for today	Where I saw/heard God
What I'm giving to God	Successes
Distractions to be aware of	Challenges
I'm grateful for	Prayer requests

Monday: AM   PM

My prayer for today	Where I saw/heard God
What I'm giving to God	Successes
Distractions to be aware of	Challenges
I'm grateful for	Prayer requests

Tuesday: AM   PM

My prayer for today	Where I saw/heard God
What I'm giving to God	Successes
Distractions to be aware of	Challenges
I'm grateful for	Prayer requests

Wednesday: AM   PM

My prayer for today	Where I saw/heard God
What I'm giving to God	Successes
Distractions to be aware of	Challenges
I'm grateful for	Prayer requests

Thursday: AM   PM

My prayer for today	Where I saw/heard God
What I'm giving to God	Successes
Distractions to be aware of	Challenges
I'm grateful for	Prayer requests

Friday: AM   PM

My prayer for today	Where I saw/heard God
What I'm giving to God	Successes
Distractions to be aware of	Challenges
I'm grateful for	Prayer requests

Saturday: AM   PM

My prayer for today	Where I saw/heard God
What I'm giving to God	Successes
Distractions to be aware of	Challenges
I'm grateful for	Prayer requests

Romans 12:9 Love must be sincere. Hate what is evil; cling to what is good.

My Focus This Week:
....
....
....
....

My Affirmation or Focus Statement:
....
....
....
....

Sunday:

AM	PM
My prayer for today	Where I saw/heard God
What I'm giving to God	Successes
Distractions to be aware of	Challenges
I'm grateful for	Prayer requests

Monday: AM | PM

My prayer for today	Where I saw/heard God
What I'm giving to God	Successes
Distractions to be aware of	Challenges
I'm grateful for	Prayer requests

Tuesday: AM | PM

My prayer for today	Where I saw/heard God
What I'm giving to God	Successes
Distractions to be aware of	Challenges
I'm grateful for	Prayer requests

Wednesday: AM   PM

My prayer for today	Where I saw/heard God
What I'm giving to God	Successes
Distractions to be aware of	Challenges
I'm grateful for	Prayer requests

Thursday: AM   PM

My prayer for today	Where I saw/heard God
What I'm giving to God	Successes
Distractions to be aware of	Challenges
I'm grateful for	Prayer requests

Friday: AM PM

My prayer for today	Where I saw/heard God
What I'm giving to God	Successes
Distractions to be aware of	Challenges
I'm grateful for	Prayer requests

Saturday: AM PM

My prayer for today	Where I saw/heard God
What I'm giving to God	Successes
Distractions to be aware of	Challenges
I'm grateful for	Prayer requests

Week Three

Philippians 4:6-7 Do not be anxious about anything, but in every situation, by prayer and petition, with thanksgiving, present your requests to God. And the peace of God, which transcends all understanding, will guard your hearts and your minds in Christ Jesus.

My Focus This Week:
....
....
....
....

My Affirmation or Focus Statement:
....
....
....
....

Sunday:

AM	PM
My prayer for today	Where I saw/heard God
What I'm giving to God	Successes
Distractions to be aware of	Challenges
I'm grateful for	Prayer requests

Monday: AM   PM

My prayer for today	Where I saw/heard God
What I'm giving to God	Successes
Distractions to be aware of	Challenges
I'm grateful for	Prayer requests

Tuesday: AM   PM

My prayer for today	Where I saw/heard God
What I'm giving to God	Successes
Distractions to be aware of	Challenges
I'm grateful for	Prayer requests

Wednesday: AM   PM

My prayer for today	Where I saw/heard God
What I'm giving to God	Successes
Distractions to be aware of	Challenges
I'm grateful for	Prayer requests

Thursday: AM   PM

My prayer for today	Where I saw/heard God
What I'm giving to God	Successes
Distractions to be aware of	Challenges
I'm grateful for	Prayer requests

Friday:　　　AM　　　　　　　　　　　PM

My prayer for today	Where I saw/heard God
What I'm giving to God	Successes
Distractions to be aware of	Challenges
I'm grateful for	Prayer requests

Saturday:　　　AM　　　　　　　　　　　PM

My prayer for today	Where I saw/heard God
What I'm giving to God	Successes
Distractions to be aware of	Challenges
I'm grateful for	Prayer requests

Psalm 5:3 In the morning, LORD, you hear my voice; in the morning I lay my requests before you and wait expectantly.

My Focus This Week:
....
....
....
....

My Affirmation or Focus Statement:
....
....
....
....

Sunday: AM PM

My prayer for today	Where I saw/heard God
What I'm giving to God	Successes
Distractions to be aware of	Challenges
I'm grateful for	Prayer requests

Monday: AM   PM

My prayer for today	Where I saw/heard God
What I'm giving to God	Successes
Distractions to be aware of	Challenges
I'm grateful for	Prayer requests

Tuesday: AM   PM

My prayer for today	Where I saw/heard God
What I'm giving to God	Successes
Distractions to be aware of	Challenges
I'm grateful for	Prayer requests

Wednesday: AM   PM

My prayer for today	Where I saw/heard God
What I'm giving to God	Successes
Distractions to be aware of	Challenges
I'm grateful for	Prayer requests

Thursday: AM   PM

My prayer for today	Where I saw/heard God
What I'm giving to God	Successes
Distractions to be aware of	Challenges
I'm grateful for	Prayer requests

Friday: AM   PM

My prayer for today	Where I saw/heard God
What I'm giving to God	Successes
Distractions to be aware of	Challenges
I'm grateful for	Prayer requests

Saturday: AM   PM

My prayer for today	Where I saw/heard God
What I'm giving to God	Successes
Distractions to be aware of	Challenges
I'm grateful for	Prayer requests

Monthly Reflection

Use this space to reflect on your previous month.

....
....
....
....
....
....
....
....
....
....
....
....
....
....
....
....
....
....
....
....
....
....
....
....
....

Month Five: Education

Would you consider yourself a lifelong learner? Why or why not? Do you have a natural curiosity to research or look further into things that pique your interest? (extra pages in back)

………………………………………………………………………………………………
………………………………………………………………………………………………
………………………………………………………………………………………………
………………………………………………………………………………………………

Think about your formal education. What from it have you used in your day-to-day life?

………………………………………………………………………………………………
………………………………………………………………………………………………
………………………………………………………………………………………………
………………………………………………………………………………………………

Did you obtain or are you working toward a spiritual education? If so, what are some things you've learned that help you day-to-day?

………………………………………………………………………………………………
………………………………………………………………………………………………
………………………………………………………………………………………………
………………………………………………………………………………………………

What are the things you'd like to know, wish you knew or knew how to do, or would like to learn more about?

………………………………………………………………………………………………
………………………………………………………………………………………………
………………………………………………………………………………………………

Verses for the Month

Write these verses by hand at the beginning of each week. Then record any thoughts, feelings or reflections that come to mind.

Week 1

Proverbs 1:7 The fear of the LORD is the beginning of knowledge, but fools despise wisdom and instruction.

....
....
....
....
....
....
....
....
....

Week 2

James 1:5 If any of you lacks wisdom, you should ask God, who gives generously to all without finding fault, and it will be given to you.

....
....
....
....
....
....
....
....
....

Week 3
Proverbs 11:14 For lack of guidance a nation falls, but victory is won through many advisers.

....
....
....
....
....
....
....
....
....

Week 4
Proverbs 18:15 The heart of the discerning acquires knowledge, for the ears of the wise seek it out.

....
....
....
....
....
....
....

How do these verses apply to your focus word for this year?

....
....
....
....
....
....

Proverbs 9:7 The fear of the LORD is the beginning of knowledge, but fools despise wisdom and instruction.

My Focus This Week:

....
....
....
....

My Affirmation or Focus Statement:

....
....
....
....

Sunday:

AM	PM
My prayer for today	Where I saw/heard God
What I'm giving to God	Successes
Distractions to be aware of	Challenges
I'm grateful for	Prayer requests

Monday: AM   PM

My prayer for today	Where I saw/heard God
What I'm giving to God	Successes
Distractions to be aware of	Challenges
I'm grateful for	Prayer requests

Tuesday: AM   PM

My prayer for today	Where I saw/heard God
What I'm giving to God	Successes
Distractions to be aware of	Challenges
I'm grateful for	Prayer requests

Wednesday: AM   PM

My prayer for today	Where I saw/heard God
What I'm giving to God	Successes
Distractions to be aware of	Challenges
I'm grateful for	Prayer requests

Thursday: AM   PM

My prayer for today	Where I saw/heard God
What I'm giving to God	Successes
Distractions to be aware of	Challenges
I'm grateful for	Prayer requests

Friday: AM PM

My prayer for today	Where I saw/heard God
What I'm giving to God	Successes
Distractions to be aware of	Challenges
I'm grateful for	Prayer requests

Saturday: AM PM

My prayer for today	Where I saw/heard God
What I'm giving to God	Successes
Distractions to be aware of	Challenges
I'm grateful for	Prayer requests

James 1:5 If any of you lacks wisdom, you should ask God, who gives generously to all without finding fault, and it will be given to you.

My Focus This Week:
....
....
....
....

My Affirmation or Focus Statement:
....
....
....
....

Sunday:

AM	PM
My prayer for today	Where I saw/heard God
What I'm giving to God	Successes
Distractions to be aware of	Challenges
I'm grateful for	Prayer requests

Monday: AM   PM

My prayer for today	Where I saw/heard God
What I'm giving to God	Successes
Distractions to be aware of	Challenges
I'm grateful for	Prayer requests

Tuesday: AM   PM

My prayer for today	Where I saw/heard God
What I'm giving to God	Successes
Distractions to be aware of	Challenges
I'm grateful for	Prayer requests

Wednesday: AM   PM

My prayer for today	Where I saw/heard God
What I'm giving to God	Successes
Distractions to be aware of	Challenges
I'm grateful for	Prayer requests

Thursday: AM   PM

My prayer for today	Where I saw/heard God
What I'm giving to God	Successes
Distractions to be aware of	Challenges
I'm grateful for	Prayer requests

Friday: AM   PM

My prayer for today	Where I saw/heard God
What I'm giving to God	Successes
Distractions to be aware of	Challenges
I'm grateful for	Prayer requests

Saturday: AM   PM

My prayer for today	Where I saw/heard God
What I'm giving to God	Successes
Distractions to be aware of	Challenges
I'm grateful for	Prayer requests

Week Three

Proverbs 11:14 For lack of guidance a nation falls, but victory is won through many advisers.

My Focus This Week:
....
....
....
....

My Affirmation or Focus Statement:
....
....
....
....

Sunday:

AM	PM
My prayer for today	Where I saw/heard God
What I'm giving to God	Successes
Distractions to be aware of	Challenges
I'm grateful for	Prayer requests

Monday: AM   PM

My prayer for today	Where I saw/heard God
What I'm giving to God	Successes
Distractions to be aware of	Challenges
I'm grateful for	Prayer requests

Tuesday: AM   PM

My prayer for today	Where I saw/heard God
What I'm giving to God	Successes
Distractions to be aware of	Challenges
I'm grateful for	Prayer requests

Wednesday: AM   PM

My prayer for today	Where I saw/heard God
What I'm giving to God	Successes
Distractions to be aware of	Challenges
I'm grateful for	Prayer requests

Thursday: AM   PM

My prayer for today	Where I saw/heard God
What I'm giving to God	Successes
Distractions to be aware of	Challenges
I'm grateful for	Prayer requests

Friday: AM   PM

My prayer for today	Where I saw/heard God
What I'm giving to God	Successes
Distractions to be aware of	Challenges
I'm grateful for	Prayer requests

Saturday: AM   PM

My prayer for today	Where I saw/heard God
What I'm giving to God	Successes
Distractions to be aware of	Challenges
I'm grateful for	Prayer requests

Week Four

Proverbs 18:15 The heart of the discerning acquires knowledge, for the ears of the wise seek it out.

My Focus This Week:

....
....
....
....

My Affirmation or Focus Statement:

....
....
....
....

Sunday:

AM	PM
My prayer for today	Where I saw/heard God
What I'm giving to God	Successes
Distractions to be aware of	Challenges
I'm grateful for	Prayer requests

Monday: AM   PM

My prayer for today	Where I saw/heard God
What I'm giving to God	Successes
Distractions to be aware of	Challenges
I'm grateful for	Prayer requests

Tuesday: AM   PM

My prayer for today	Where I saw/heard God
What I'm giving to God	Successes
Distractions to be aware of	Challenges
I'm grateful for	Prayer requests

Wednesday: AM   PM

My prayer for today	Where I saw/heard God
What I'm giving to God	Successes
Distractions to be aware of	Challenges
I'm grateful for	Prayer requests

Thursday: AM   PM

My prayer for today	Where I saw/heard God
What I'm giving to God	Successes
Distractions to be aware of	Challenges
I'm grateful for	Prayer requests

Friday: AM   PM

My prayer for today	Where I saw/heard God
What I'm giving to God	Successes
Distractions to be aware of	Challenges
I'm grateful for	Prayer requests

Saturday: AM   PM

My prayer for today	Where I saw/heard God
What I'm giving to God	Successes
Distractions to be aware of	Challenges
I'm grateful for	Prayer requests

Monthly Reflection

Use this space to reflect on your previous month.

....
....
....
....
....
....
....
....
....
....
....
....
....
....
....
....
....
....
....
....
....
....
....
....
....
....

Month Six: Family

Family is a blessing, but it can be the cause of our deepest joy and greatest stress. If we remember Romans 8:28, we know that God has placed us purposefully. We may not feel we're in the right place or with the right people, but if we embrace God's Plan, we can find beauty and joy in it when we love unconditionally, as God loves us.

That said, it's important to set and enforce boundaries if relationships become toxic or unhealthy. We need to always put our own oxygen mask on first before we help others.

If you have children, you may be familiar with "train up your children in the way they should go." Have you ever unpacked that verse? Notice how it says the way they should go—not the way you want them to go. God has created them for a purpose, and if you push your ideas and expectations too hard, they could miss or never discover their purpose. We know what it's like when we're not on the right path—life is hard, painful, and full of strife. It's the same for our kids. Encourage their interests, help them amplify their strengths, and nurture them to voice their insights, passions, and desires.

Remember, we can't change people. We can only love them. God made them, and only He can change and open hearts.

Reflect on your family relationships. Do you wish any were different? If so, I challenge you to find goodness in a challenging person or relationship. Pray about it. Reach out. And let God work. (pages in back)

....
....
....
....
....
....
....
....

Verses for the Month

Write these verses by hand at the beginning of each week. Then record any thoughts, feelings, or reflections that come to mind.

Week 1

Ephesians 4:32 Be kind and compassionate to one another, forgiving each other, just as in Christ God forgave you.

....
....
....
....
....
....
....
....
....
....

Week 2

James 1:19 My dear brothers and sisters, take note of this: Everyone should be quick to listen, slow to speak and slow to become angry.

....
....
....
....
....
....
....
....
....
....

Week 3

Colossians 3:13 Bear with each other and forgive one another if any of you has a grievance against someone. Forgive as the Lord forgave you.

....
....
....
....
....
....

Week 4

1 Corinthians 13:4-8 Love is patient, love is kind. It does not envy, it does not boast, it is not proud. It does not dishonor others, it is not self-seeking, it is not easily angered, it keeps no record of wrongs. Love does not delight in evil but rejoices with the truth. It always protects, always trusts, always hopes, always perseveres. Love never fails. But where there are prophecies, they will cease; where there are tongues, they will be stilled; where there is knowledge, it will pass away.

....
....
....
....
....
....
....

How do these verses apply to your focus word for this year?

....
....
....
....

Ephesians 4:32 Be kind and compassionate to one another, forgiving each other, just as in Christ God forgave you.

My Focus This Week:
....
....
....
....

My Affirmation or Focus Statement:
....
....
....
....

Sunday:

AM	PM
My prayer for today	Where I saw/heard God
What I'm giving to God	Successes
Distractions to be aware of	Challenges
I'm grateful for	Prayer requests

Monday: AM   PM

My prayer for today	Where I saw/heard God
What I'm giving to God	Successes
Distractions to be aware of	Challenges
I'm grateful for	Prayer requests

Tuesday: AM   PM

My prayer for today	Where I saw/heard God
What I'm giving to God	Successes
Distractions to be aware of	Challenges
I'm grateful for	Prayer requests

Wednesday: AM   PM

My prayer for today	Where I saw/heard God
What I'm giving to God	Successes
Distractions to be aware of	Challenges
I'm grateful for	Prayer requests

Thursday: AM   PM

My prayer for today	Where I saw/heard God
What I'm giving to God	Successes
Distractions to be aware of	Challenges
I'm grateful for	Prayer requests

Friday: AM   PM

My prayer for today	Where I saw/heard God
What I'm giving to God	Successes
Distractions to be aware of	Challenges
I'm grateful for	Prayer requests

Saturday: AM   PM

My prayer for today	Where I saw/heard God
What I'm giving to God	Successes
Distractions to be aware of	Challenges
I'm grateful for	Prayer requests

James 1:19 My dear brothers and sisters, take note of this: Everyone should be quick to listen, slow to speak and slow to become angry.

My Focus This Week:
....
....
....
....

My Affirmation or Focus Statement:
....
....
....
....

Sunday:

AM	PM
My prayer for today	Where I saw/heard God
What I'm giving to God	Successes
Distractions to be aware of	Challenges
I'm grateful for	Prayer requests

Monday: AM   PM

My prayer for today	Where I saw/heard God
What I'm giving to God	Successes
Distractions to be aware of	Challenges
I'm grateful for	Prayer requests

Tuesday: AM   PM

My prayer for today	Where I saw/heard God
What I'm giving to God	Successes
Distractions to be aware of	Challenges
I'm grateful for	Prayer requests

Wednesday: AM   PM

My prayer for today	Where I saw/heard God
What I'm giving to God	Successes
Distractions to be aware of	Challenges
I'm grateful for	Prayer requests

Thursday: AM   PM

My prayer for today	Where I saw/heard God
What I'm giving to God	Successes
Distractions to be aware of	Challenges
I'm grateful for	Prayer requests

Friday: AM   PM

My prayer for today	Where I saw/heard God
What I'm giving to God	Successes
Distractions to be aware of	Challenges
I'm grateful for	Prayer requests

Saturday: AM   PM

My prayer for today	Where I saw/heard God
What I'm giving to God	Successes
Distractions to be aware of	Challenges
I'm grateful for	Prayer requests

Colossians 3:13 Bear with each other and forgive one another if any of you has a grievance against someone. Forgive as the Lord forgave you.

My Focus This Week:
....
....
....
....

My Affirmation or Focus Statement:
....
....
....
....

Sunday:

AM	PM
My prayer for today	Where I saw/heard God
What I'm giving to God	Successes
Distractions to be aware of	Challenges
I'm grateful for	Prayer requests

Monday: AM   PM

My prayer for today	Where I saw/heard God
What I'm giving to God	Successes
Distractions to be aware of	Challenges
I'm grateful for	Prayer requests

Tuesday: AM   PM

My prayer for today	Where I saw/heard God
What I'm giving to God	Successes
Distractions to be aware of	Challenges
I'm grateful for	Prayer requests

Wednesday: AM   PM

AM	PM
My prayer for today	Where I saw/heard God
What I'm giving to God	Successes
Distractions to be aware of	Challenges
I'm grateful for	Prayer requests

Thursday: AM   PM

AM	PM
My prayer for today	Where I saw/heard God
What I'm giving to God	Successes
Distractions to be aware of	Challenges
I'm grateful for	Prayer requests

Friday: AM PM

My prayer for today	Where I saw/heard God

What I'm giving to God	Successes

Distractions to be aware of	Challenges

I'm grateful for	Prayer requests

Saturday: AM PM

My prayer for today	Where I saw/heard God

What I'm giving to God	Successes

Distractions to be aware of	Challenges

I'm grateful for	Prayer requests

1 Corinthians 13:1-8 Love is patient, love is kind. It does not envy, it does not boast, it is not proud. It does not dishonor others, it is not self-seeking, it is not easily angered, it keeps no record of wrongs. Love does not delight in evil but rejoices with the truth. It always protects, always trusts, always hopes, always perseveres. Love never fails. But where there are prophecies, they will cease; where there are tongues, they will be stilled; where there is knowledge, it will pass away.

My Focus This Week:

....
....
....
....

My Affirmation or Focus Statement:

....
....
....
....

Sunday:

AM	PM
My prayer for today	Where I saw/heard God
What I'm giving to God	Successes
Distractions to be aware of	Challenges
I'm grateful for	Prayer requests

Monday: AM   PM

My prayer for today	Where I saw/heard God
What I'm giving to God	Successes
Distractions to be aware of	Challenges
I'm grateful for	Prayer requests

Tuesday: AM   PM

My prayer for today	Where I saw/heard God
What I'm giving to God	Successes
Distractions to be aware of	Challenges
I'm grateful for	Prayer requests

Wednesday: AM PM

My prayer for today	Where I saw/heard God
What I'm giving to God	Successes
Distractions to be aware of	Challenges
I'm grateful for	Prayer requests

Thursday: AM PM

My prayer for today	Where I saw/heard God
What I'm giving to God	Successes
Distractions to be aware of	Challenges
I'm grateful for	Prayer requests

Friday: AM   PM

My prayer for today	Where I saw/heard God
What I'm giving to God	Successes
Distractions to be aware of	Challenges
I'm grateful for	Prayer requests

Saturday: AM   PM

My prayer for today	Where I saw/heard God
What I'm giving to God	Successes
Distractions to be aware of	Challenges
I'm grateful for	Prayer requests

Monthly Reflection

Use this space to reflect on your previous month.

....
....
....
....
....
....
....
....
....
....
....
....
....
....
....
....
....
....
....
....
....
....
....
....
....
....

Quarterly Reflection

Proverbs 13:22 **A good person leaves an inheritance for their children's children, but a sinner's wealth is stored up for the righteous.**

Reflect on this and how it relates to your life and experiences.

....
....
....
....
....
....
....
....
....
....
....
....
....
....
....
....
....
....
....
....
....
....
....

Answered Prayers

What prayers did God answer this quarter?

Month Seven: Friendships

In life, we have many friendships. God programmed us for community. We're internally wired for village mentality, and even the most introverted among us need people and need to feel loved and valued.

Have you considered Jesus as one of your friends? Do you talk to him every day? I encourage you to do so, whether out loud or through journaling. Oftentimes, hearing or seeing our words offers another level of comprehension and helps us clarify thoughts, inform ideas, and solve problems.

Some people come into our lives for a season, some briefly to teach us a lesson, and others forever. It's important to choose friends who pull you toward the light instead of the dark. That said, we can't all be positive and strong all the time. Supporting others in times of need or weakness is what Jesus would do, and having a community of support is essential to our wellbeing.

Do you have a core group of friends? You are the average of the five people closest to you. Are they pushing you up or down? Can you be honest with them and can they be honest with you?

Evaluate your friendships. See the four concentric circles on the next page? In the center, list your core friends. These are the people you can call anytime, for anything and they'll move heaven and earth to be there for you. The next circle is you clique. This is a handful of people you spend the most time with and trust, but they might not know your deepest secrets. The third circle is your crowd—a good number of people who are important to you. You'd invite them to your most significant events and enjoy spending time with them. The outer circle is your community—neighbors, colleagues, co-workers, and other acquaintances.

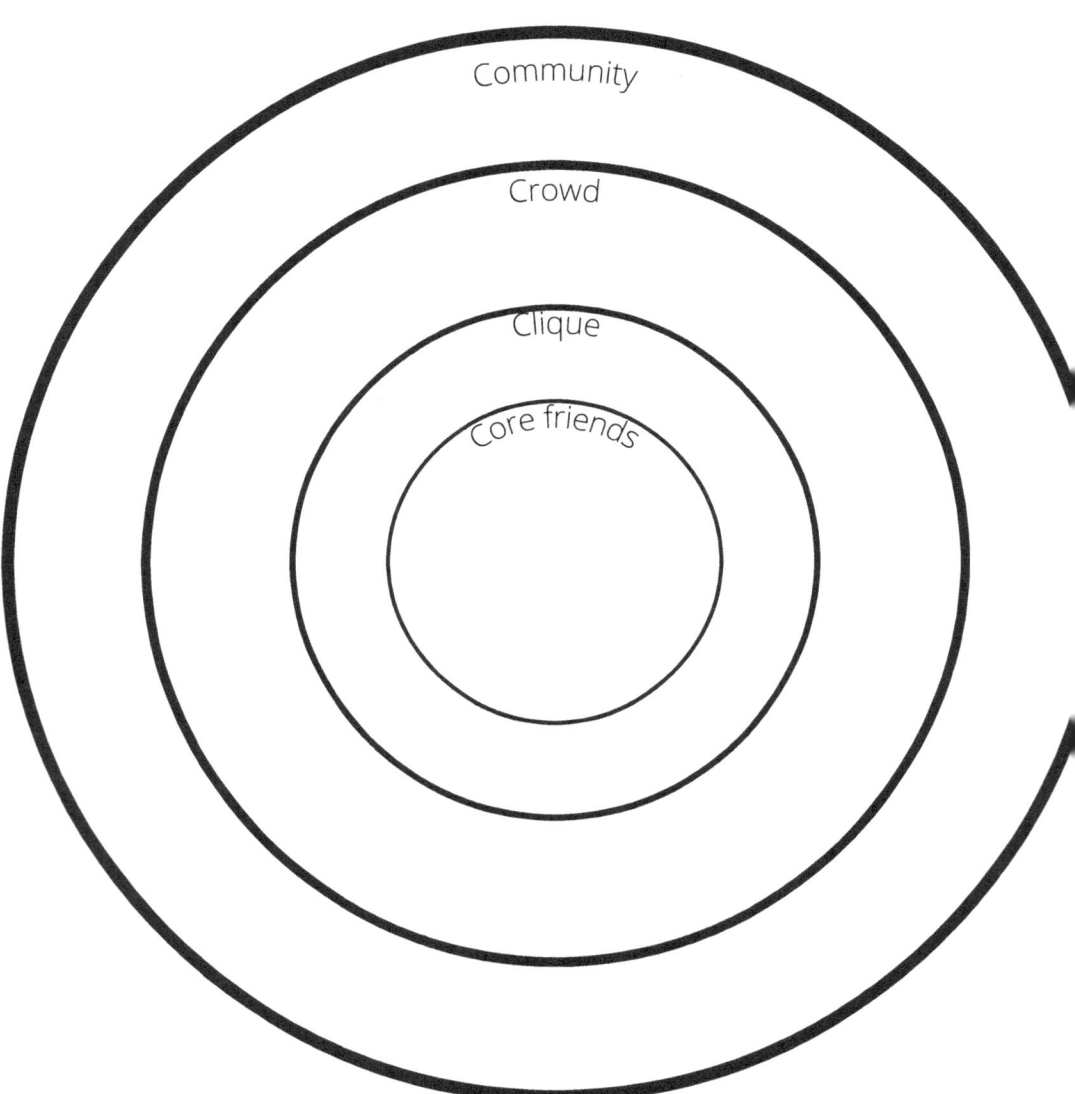

Do your circles represent the friendships you'd like to have? Do you have too little or too many in certain circles? What steps can you take to refine your friendships?

Verses for the Month

Write these verses by hand at the beginning of each week. Then record any thoughts, feelings, or reflections that come to mind.

Week 1

Proverbs 4:23 Above all else, guard your heart, for everything you do flows from it.

....
....
....
....
....
....
....
....
....
....

Week 2

Luke 6:27-28 But to you who are listening I say: Love your enemies, do good to those who hate you, bless those who curse you, pray for those who mistreat you.

....
....
....
....
....
....
....
....
....
....

Week 3
Galatians 6:2 Carry each other's burdens, and in this way, you will fulfill the law of Christ.

....
....
....
....
....
....
....
....
....

Week 4
Luke 6:31 Do to others as you would have them do to you.

....
....
....
....
....
....
....
....

How do these verses apply to your focus word for this year?

....
....
....
....
....
....

Week One

Proverbs 4:23 Above all else, guard your heart, for everything you do flows from it.

My Focus This Week:
....
....
....
....

My Affirmation or Focus Statement:
....
....
....
....

Sunday:

AM	PM
My prayer for today	Where I saw/heard God
What I'm giving to God	Successes
Distractions to be aware of	Challenges
I'm grateful for	Prayer requests

Monday: AM   PM

My prayer for today	Where I saw/heard God
What I'm giving to God	Successes
Distractions to be aware of	Challenges
I'm grateful for	Prayer requests

Tuesday: AM   PM

My prayer for today	Where I saw/heard God
What I'm giving to God	Successes
Distractions to be aware of	Challenges
I'm grateful for	Prayer requests

Wednesday: AM   PM

AM	PM
My prayer for today	Where I saw/heard God
What I'm giving to God	Successes
Distractions to be aware of	Challenges
I'm grateful for	Prayer requests

Thursday: AM   PM

AM	PM
My prayer for today	Where I saw/heard God
What I'm giving to God	Successes
Distractions to be aware of	Challenges
I'm grateful for	Prayer requests

Friday: AM　　　　　　　　　　　PM

My prayer for today	Where I saw/heard God

What I'm giving to God	Successes

Distractions to be aware of	Challenges

I'm grateful for	Prayer requests

Saturday: AM　　　　　　　　　　PM

My prayer for today	Where I saw/heard God

What I'm giving to God	Successes

Distractions to be aware of	Challenges

I'm grateful for	Prayer requests

Week Two

Luke 6:27-28 "But to you who are listening I say: Love your enemies, do good to those who hate you, bless those who curse you, pray for those who mistreat you."

My Focus This Week:
....
....
....
....

My Affirmation or Focus Statement:
....
....
....
....

Sunday:

AM	PM
My prayer for today	Where I saw/heard God
What I'm giving to God	Successes
Distractions to be aware of	Challenges
I'm grateful for	Prayer requests

Monday: AM   PM

My prayer for today	Where I saw/heard God
What I'm giving to God	Successes
Distractions to be aware of	Challenges
I'm grateful for	Prayer requests

Tuesday: AM   PM

My prayer for today	Where I saw/heard God
What I'm giving to God	Successes
Distractions to be aware of	Challenges
I'm grateful for	Prayer requests

Wednesday: AM   PM

My prayer for today	Where I saw/heard God
What I'm giving to God	Successes
Distractions to be aware of	Challenges
I'm grateful for	Prayer requests

Thursday: AM   PM

My prayer for today	Where I saw/heard God
What I'm giving to God	Successes
Distractions to be aware of	Challenges
I'm grateful for	Prayer requests

Friday: AM   PM

My prayer for today	Where I saw/heard God
What I'm giving to God	Successes
Distractions to be aware of	Challenges
I'm grateful for	Prayer requests

Saturday: AM   PM

My prayer for today	Where I saw/heard God
What I'm giving to God	Successes
Distractions to be aware of	Challenges
I'm grateful for	Prayer requests

Week Three

Galatians 6:2 Carry each other's burdens, and in this way, you will fulfill the law of Christ.

My Focus This Week:
....
....
....
....

My Affirmation or Focus Statement:
....
....
....
....

Sunday:

AM	PM
My prayer for today	Where I saw/heard God
What I'm giving to God	Successes
Distractions to be aware of	Challenges
I'm grateful for	Prayer requests

Monday: AM   PM

My prayer for today	Where I saw/heard God
What I'm giving to God	Successes
Distractions to be aware of	Challenges
I'm grateful for	Prayer requests

Tuesday: AM   PM

My prayer for today	Where I saw/heard God
What I'm giving to God	Successes
Distractions to be aware of	Challenges
I'm grateful for	Prayer requests

Wednesday: AM   PM

My prayer for today	Where I saw/heard God
What I'm giving to God	Successes
Distractions to be aware of	Challenges
I'm grateful for	Prayer requests

Thursday: AM   PM

My prayer for today	Where I saw/heard God
What I'm giving to God	Successes
Distractions to be aware of	Challenges
I'm grateful for	Prayer requests

Friday: AM   PM

My prayer for today	Where I saw/heard God
What I'm giving to God	Successes
Distractions to be aware of	Challenges
I'm grateful for	Prayer requests

Saturday: AM   PM

My prayer for today	Where I saw/heard God
What I'm giving to God	Successes
Distractions to be aware of	Challenges
I'm grateful for	Prayer requests

Luke 6:31 Do to others as you would have them do to you.

Week Four

My Focus This Week:

....
....
....
....

My Affirmation or Focus Statement:

....
....
....
....

Sunday:

AM	PM
My prayer for today	Where I saw/heard God
What I'm giving to God	Successes
Distractions to be aware of	Challenges
I'm grateful for	Prayer requests

Monday: AM PM

My prayer for today	Where I saw/heard God
What I'm giving to God	Successes
Distractions to be aware of	Challenges
I'm grateful for	Prayer requests

Tuesday: AM PM

My prayer for today	Where I saw/heard God
What I'm giving to God	Successes
Distractions to be aware of	Challenges
I'm grateful for	Prayer requests

Wednesday: AM — PM

My prayer for today	Where I saw/heard God
What I'm giving to God	Successes
Distractions to be aware of	Challenges
I'm grateful for	Prayer requests

Thursday: AM — PM

My prayer for today	Where I saw/heard God
What I'm giving to God	Successes
Distractions to be aware of	Challenges
I'm grateful for	Prayer requests

Friday: AM   PM

My prayer for today	Where I saw/heard God
What I'm giving to God	Successes
Distractions to be aware of	Challenges
I'm grateful for	Prayer requests

Saturday: AM   PM

My prayer for today	Where I saw/heard God
What I'm giving to God	Successes
Distractions to be aware of	Challenges
I'm grateful for	Prayer requests

Monthly Reflection

Use this space to reflect on your previous month.

....
....
....
....
....
....
....
....
....
....
....
....
....
....
....
....
....
....
....
....
....
....
....
....
....
....
....
....
....

Month Eight: Personal Success

In our pursuit of success, we often lose sight of what success is. Success may have meant getting into a good college, then getting a high-paying or prestigious job, having a couple of kids to repeat your success, and then retire and relax.

I challenge that SO HARD. It's too status quo. While that may be the life it looks like I'm living, especially if you're on the outside looking in, it's not. Not since I started listening to God. A homeschool mom friend told me once she was raising her kids to be heaven-bound, not Harvard-bound. That was a gut punch. But as I thought about it, it's what God wants for me that will ultimately lead me to my success. He designed me. He knows what I'm good at, what I like and what I don't, and everything else about me. He designed me with a talent for teaching and a gift of creativity. I could probably work as an accountant or lawyer or doctor, but I'd be miserable. I don't have a natural aptitude for numbers, argument, or science. It would be a struggle to try to be someone I'm not.

I pose a question: is my orthopedic surgeon more successful than I am, a writer who has yet to make as much as she has invested into her business? If you said yes, write down why you think that. Is it money or prestige that led to your affirmative answer? If you said no, write down why.

I'm in the *no* camp on this one. I'd say we are equally successful if we both enjoy our job and are positively impacting others and improving their quality of life. And most of all—if we enjoy what we do, we're on the path God laid out for us when He created us.

Think about what success means to you. Journal your ultimate goals and what getting there costs you. Money? Time with your family? Is it worth it? Happiness? If it is, congrats! If it's not, challenge your personal expectations and those you put on others. (extra pages in back)

....
....
....
....
....
....

Verses for the Month

Write these verses by hand at the beginning of each week. Then record any thoughts, feelings, or reflections that come to mind.

Week 1

Hebrews 12:11 No discipline seems pleasant at the time, but painful. Later on, however, it produces a harvest of righteousness and peace for those who have been trained by it.

....
....
....
....
....
....
....
....
....

Week 2

Colossians 3:23 Whatever you do, work at it with all your heart, as working for the Lord, not for human masters.

....
....
....
....
....
....
....
....
....

Week 3

Proverbs 16:3 Commit to the LORD whatever you do, and He will establish your plans.

....
....
....
....
....
....
....
....
....

Week 4

Ecclesiastes 5:10 Whoever loves money never has enough; whoever loves wealth is never satisfied with their income. This too is meaningless.

....
....
....
....
....
....
....

How do these verses apply to your focus word for this year?

....
....
....
....
....

Hebrews 12:11 No discipline seems pleasant at the time, but painful. Later on, however, it produces a harvest of righteousness and peace for those who have been trained by it.

My Focus This Week:
....
....
....
....

My Affirmation or Focus Statement:
....
....
....
....

Sunday: AM PM

My prayer for today	Where I saw/heard God
What I'm giving to God	Successes
Distractions to be aware of	Challenges
I'm grateful for	Prayer requests

Monday: AM   PM

My prayer for today	Where I saw/heard God
What I'm giving to God	Successes
Distractions to be aware of	Challenges
I'm grateful for	Prayer requests

Tuesday: AM   PM

My prayer for today	Where I saw/heard God
What I'm giving to God	Successes
Distractions to be aware of	Challenges
I'm grateful for	Prayer requests

Wednesday: AM   PM

My prayer for today	Where I saw/heard God
What I'm giving to God	Successes
Distractions to be aware of	Challenges
I'm grateful for	Prayer requests

Thursday: AM   PM

My prayer for today	Where I saw/heard God
What I'm giving to God	Successes
Distractions to be aware of	Challenges
I'm grateful for	Prayer requests

Friday: AM   PM

My prayer for today	Where I saw/heard God
What I'm giving to God	Successes
Distractions to be aware of	Challenges
I'm grateful for	Prayer requests

Saturday: AM   PM

My prayer for today	Where I saw/heard God
What I'm giving to God	Successes
Distractions to be aware of	Challenges
I'm grateful for	Prayer requests

Week Two

Colossians 3:23 Whatever you do, work at it with all your heart, as working for the Lord, not for human masters.

My Focus This Week:

....
....
....
....

My Affirmation or Focus Statement:

....
....
....
....

Sunday: AM / PM

My prayer for today	Where I saw/heard God
What I'm giving to God	Successes
Distractions to be aware of	Challenges
I'm grateful for	Prayer requests

Monday: AM PM

My prayer for today	Where I saw/heard God
What I'm giving to God	Successes
Distractions to be aware of	Challenges
I'm grateful for	Prayer requests

Tuesday: AM PM

My prayer for today	Where I saw/heard God
What I'm giving to God	Successes
Distractions to be aware of	Challenges
I'm grateful for	Prayer requests

Wednesday: AM   PM

My prayer for today	Where I saw/heard God
What I'm giving to God	Successes
Distractions to be aware of	Challenges
I'm grateful for	Prayer requests

Thursday: AM   PM

My prayer for today	Where I saw/heard God
What I'm giving to God	Successes
Distractions to be aware of	Challenges
I'm grateful for	Prayer requests

Friday: AM   PM

My prayer for today	Where I saw/heard God
What I'm giving to God	Successes
Distractions to be aware of	Challenges
I'm grateful for	Prayer requests

Saturday: AM   PM

My prayer for today	Where I saw/heard God
What I'm giving to God	Successes
Distractions to be aware of	Challenges
I'm grateful for	Prayer requests

Proverbs 16:3 Commit to the LORD whatever you do, and He will establish your plans.

My Focus This Week:
....
....
....
....

My Affirmation or Focus Statement:
....
....
....
....

Sunday:

AM	PM
My prayer for today	Where I saw/heard God
What I'm giving to God	Successes
Distractions to be aware of	Challenges
I'm grateful for	Prayer requests

Monday: AM · PM

My prayer for today	Where I saw/heard God
What I'm giving to God	Successes
Distractions to be aware of	Challenges
I'm grateful for	Prayer requests

Tuesday: AM · PM

My prayer for today	Where I saw/heard God
What I'm giving to God	Successes
Distractions to be aware of	Challenges
I'm grateful for	Prayer requests

Wednesday: AM   PM

My prayer for today	Where I saw/heard God
What I'm giving to God	Successes
Distractions to be aware of	Challenges
I'm grateful for	Prayer requests

Thursday: AM   PM

My prayer for today	Where I saw/heard God
What I'm giving to God	Successes
Distractions to be aware of	Challenges
I'm grateful for	Prayer requests

Friday: AM   PM

My prayer for today	Where I saw/heard God
What I'm giving to God	Successes
Distractions to be aware of	Challenges
I'm grateful for	Prayer requests

Saturday: AM   PM

My prayer for today	Where I saw/heard God
What I'm giving to God	Successes
Distractions to be aware of	Challenges
I'm grateful for	Prayer requests

Ecclesiastes 5:10 Whoever loves money never has enough; whoever loves wealth is never satisfied with their income. This too is meaningless.

My Focus This Week:
....
....
....
....

My Affirmation or Focus Statement:
....
....
....
....

Sunday:

AM	PM
My prayer for today	Where I saw/heard God
What I'm giving to God	Successes
Distractions to be aware of	Challenges
I'm grateful for	Prayer requests

Monday: AM | PM

My prayer for today	Where I saw/heard God
What I'm giving to God	Successes
Distractions to be aware of	Challenges
I'm grateful for	Prayer requests

Tuesday: AM | PM

My prayer for today	Where I saw/heard God
What I'm giving to God	Successes
Distractions to be aware of	Challenges
I'm grateful for	Prayer requests

Wednesday: AM   PM

My prayer for today	Where I saw/heard God
What I'm giving to God	Successes
Distractions to be aware of	Challenges
I'm grateful for	Prayer requests

Thursday: AM   PM

My prayer for today	Where I saw/heard God
What I'm giving to God	Successes
Distractions to be aware of	Challenges
I'm grateful for	Prayer requests

Friday: AM   PM

My prayer for today	Where I saw/heard God
What I'm giving to God	Successes
Distractions to be aware of	Challenges
I'm grateful for	Prayer requests

Saturday: AM   PM

My prayer for today	Where I saw/heard God
What I'm giving to God	Successes
Distractions to be aware of	Challenges
I'm grateful for	Prayer requests

Monthly Reflection

Use this space to reflect on your previous month.

....
....
....
....
....
....
....
....
....
....
....
....
....
....
....
....
....
....
....
....
....
....
....
....

Month Nine: Service & Philanthropy

God has called us to live a life of service. He's tasked us to take care of the young, the old, the sick, and the weak, not just our own family and friends, even though at times that's all we can handle, and that's okay. He says what we do for the least among us, we do for Him. In Jesus's Sermon on the Mount, He detailed these instructions in the Book of Matthew:

3 "Blessed are the poor in spirit,
  for theirs is the kingdom of heaven.
4 Blessed are those who mourn,
  for they will be comforted.
5 Blessed are the meek,
  for they will inherit the earth.
6 Blessed are those who hunger and thirst for righteousness,
  for they will be filled.
7 Blessed are the merciful,
  for they will be shown mercy.
8 Blessed are the pure in heart,
  for they will see God.
9 Blessed are the peacemakers,
  for they will be called children of God.
10 Blessed are those who are persecuted because of righteousness,
  for theirs is the kingdom of heaven"

The people are blessed because they have God and their community to support them in all that they lack. We all lacked something at one time or another. How good is our God that He sends us help and compels us to pay it forward? Refusing assistance is refusing God. If this is an issue for you, let your pride go and take a leap of faith.

On our walk with God, we can't truly experience His goodness and light if we aren't serving others. Some may call it selfish, because there is always personal gain, whether it be a physical reward or personal joy. But this is how it's meant to be. On the most basic chemical level, the endorphins fuel us to want to do it again and again. This, my friends, is what makes our world a better place. Reach out to a friend in need, volunteer to serve the homeless or fill a Blessing Bag, or organize a food or clothing drive. One person can—and does—make a difference, every day!

How do you feel when you serve others, and though them, Him? Do you feel closer to God when you help His people? How can you do more for others?

....
....
....

Verses for the Month

Write these verses by hand at the beginning of each week. Then record any thoughts, feelings, or reflections that come to mind.

Week 1
Matthew 5:14-16 You are the light of the world. A town built on a hill cannot be hidden. Neither do people light a lamp and put it under a bowl. Instead, they put it on its stand, and it gives light to everyone in the house. In the same way, let your light shine before others, that they may see your good deeds and glorify your Father in heaven.

....
....
....
....
....
....
....
....
....

Week 2
2 Corinthians 9:7 Each of you should give what you have decided in your heart to give, not reluctantly or under compulsion, for God loves a cheerful giver.

....
....
....
....
....
....
....
....

Week 3
1 Peter 4:10 Each of you should use whatever gift you have received to serve others, as faithful stewards of God's grace in its various forms.

....
....
....
....
....
....
....
....
....

Week 4
1 John 4:19 We love because He first loved us.

....
....
....
....
....
....
....

How do these verses apply to your focus word fcr this year?

....
....
....
....
....

Week One

Matthew 5:14-16 You are the light of the world. A town built on a hill cannot be hidden. Neither do people light a lamp and put it under a bowl. Instead, they put it on its stand, and it gives light to everyone in the house. In the same way, let your light shine before others, that they may see your good deeds and glorify your Father in heaven.

My Focus This Week:

....
....
....
....

My Affirmation or Focus Statement:

....
....
....
....

Sunday:

AM	PM
My prayer for today	Where I saw/heard God
What I'm giving to God	Successes
Distractions to be aware of	Challenges
I'm grateful for	Prayer requests

Monday: AM   PM

My prayer for today	Where I saw/heard God
What I'm giving to God	Successes
Distractions to be aware of	Challenges
I'm grateful for	Prayer requests

Tuesday: AM   PM

My prayer for today	Where I saw/heard God
What I'm giving to God	Successes
Distractions to be aware of	Challenges
I'm grateful for	Prayer requests

Wednesday: AM PM

My prayer for today	Where I saw/heard God
What I'm giving to God	Successes
Distractions to be aware of	Challenges
I'm grateful for	Prayer requests

Thursday: AM PM

My prayer for today	Where I saw/heard God
What I'm giving to God	Successes
Distractions to be aware of	Challenges
I'm grateful for	Prayer requests

Friday: AM | PM

My prayer for today	Where I saw/heard God
What I'm giving to God	Successes
Distractions to be aware of	Challenges
I'm grateful for	Prayer requests

Saturday: AM | PM

My prayer for today	Where I saw/heard God
What I'm giving to God	Successes
Distractions to be aware of	Challenges
I'm grateful for	Prayer requests

2 Corinthians 9:7 Each of you should give what you have decided in your heart to give, not reluctantly or under compulsion, for God loves a cheerful giver.

My Focus This Week:
....
....
....
....

My Affirmation or Focus Statement:
....
....
....
....

Sunday:

AM	PM
My prayer for today	Where I saw/heard God
What I'm giving to God	Successes
Distractions to be aware of	Challenges
I'm grateful for	Prayer requests

Monday: AM   PM

My prayer for today	Where I saw/heard God
What I'm giving to God	Successes
Distractions to be aware of	Challenges
I'm grateful for	Prayer requests

Tuesday: AM   PM

My prayer for today	Where I saw/heard God
What I'm giving to God	Successes
Distractions to be aware of	Challenges
I'm grateful for	Prayer requests

Wednesday: AM   PM

My prayer for today	Where I saw/heard God
What I'm giving to God	Successes
Distractions to be aware of	Challenges
I'm grateful for	Prayer requests

Thursday: AM   PM

My prayer for today	Where I saw/heard God
What I'm giving to God	Successes
Distractions to be aware of	Challenges
I'm grateful for	Prayer requests

Friday: AM   PM

AM	PM
My prayer for today	Where I saw/heard God
What I'm giving to God	Successes
Distractions to be aware of	Challenges
I'm grateful for	Prayer requests

Saturday: AM   PM

AM	PM
My prayer for today	Where I saw/heard God
What I'm giving to God	Successes
Distractions to be aware of	Challenges
I'm grateful for	Prayer requests

1 Peter 4:10 Each of you should use whatever gift you have received to serve others, as faithful stewards of God's grace in its various forms.

My Focus This Week:
....
....
....
....

My Affirmation or Focus Statement:
....
....
....
....

Sunday:

AM | PM

My prayer for today	Where I saw/heard God
What I'm giving to God	Successes
Distractions to be aware of	Challenges
I'm grateful for	Prayer requests

Monday: AM   PM

My prayer for today	Where I saw/heard God
What I'm giving to God	Successes
Distractions to be aware of	Challenges
I'm grateful for	Prayer requests

Tuesday: AM   PM

My prayer for today	Where I saw/heard God
What I'm giving to God	Successes
Distractions to be aware of	Challenges
I'm grateful for	Prayer requests

Wednesday: AM   PM

My prayer for today	Where I saw/heard God
What I'm giving to God	Successes
Distractions to be aware of	Challenges
I'm grateful for	Prayer requests

Thursday: AM   PM

My prayer for today	Where I saw/heard God
What I'm giving to God	Successes
Distractions to be aware of	Challenges
I'm grateful for	Prayer requests

Friday: AM   PM

My prayer for today	Where I saw/heard God
What I'm giving to God	Successes
Distractions to be aware of	Challenges
I'm grateful for	Prayer requests

Saturday: AM   PM

My prayer for today	Where I saw/heard God
What I'm giving to God	Successes
Distractions to be aware of	Challenges
I'm grateful for	Prayer requests

Week Four

1 John 4:19 We love because He first loved us.

My Focus This Week:
....
....
....
....

My Affirmation or Focus Statement:
....
....
....
....

Sunday:

AM	PM
My prayer for today	Where I saw/heard God
What I'm giving to God	Successes
Distractions to be aware of	Challenges
I'm grateful for	Prayer requests

Monday: AM | PM

My prayer for today	Where I saw/heard God
What I'm giving to God	Successes
Distractions to be aware of	Challenges
I'm grateful for	Prayer requests

Tuesday: AM | PM

My prayer for today	Where I saw/heard God
What I'm giving to God	Successes
Distractions to be aware of	Challenges
I'm grateful for	Prayer requests

Wednesday: AM   PM

My prayer for today	Where I saw/heard God
What I'm giving to God	Successes
Distractions to be aware of	Challenges
I'm grateful for	Prayer requests

Thursday: AM   PM

My prayer for today	Where I saw/heard God
What I'm giving to God	Successes
Distractions to be aware of	Challenges
I'm grateful for	Prayer requests

Friday: AM   PM

My prayer for today	Where I saw/heard God
What I'm giving to God	Successes
Distractions to be aware of	Challenges
I'm grateful for	Prayer requests

Saturday: AM   PM

My prayer for today	Where I saw/heard God
What I'm giving to God	Successes
Distractions to be aware of	Challenges
I'm grateful for	Prayer requests

Monthly Reflection

Use this space to reflect on your previous month.

....
....
....
....
....
....
....
....
....
....
....
....
....
....
....
....
....
....
....
....
....
....
....
....
....

Quarterly Reflection

Proverbs 11:25 **A generous person will prosper; whoever refreshes others will be refreshed.**

Reflect on this and how it relates to your life and experiences.

Answered Prayers

What prayers did God answer this quarter?

Month Ten: Finance

Contrary to the popular sentiment, money is not the root of all evil. Idolatry is. Putting money, greed, power, status, etc. before God are the big no-no's. Money, on the other hand, is necessary. Currency has always been a means for survival. We can't do it all, friends. If we spend our day farming, we can't be hunting, sewing, cooking, canning, teaching our kids, traveling, caring for animals, etc, unless we have a team of people helping us. And even then, we have to pay them. Room, board, love, etc—everything is a trade.

In today's world, money talks. Without it, we're destitute. Without it, we can die. Without it, we can't help others.

Having money is a good thing! But, the more we have, the more responsibility we have to be a good steward with it. If God is providing us with more than what we need, it's our duty to help others.

Money is a tool—a resource for survival and to enable us to live out God's plan for us. We are called to provide for future generations as well, and we can't do that if we don't have a plan.

Briefly jot down your monthly income and expenses. Are you living too tightly or are you over? What steps can you take right now to balance and/or simplify your finances to be a better steward of your money and fund what you're called to do? (extra pages in back)

....
....
....
....
....
....
....
....

Verses for the Month

Write these verses by hand at the beginning of each week. Then record any thoughts, feelings, or reflections that come to mind.

Week 1
Hebrews 13:5 Keep your lives free from the love of money and be content with what you have, because God has said, "Never will I leave you; never will I forsake you."

....
....
....
....
....
....
....
....
....

Week 2
Proverbs 21:5 The plans of the diligent lead to profit as surely as haste leads to poverty.

....
....
....
....
....
....
....
....
....

Week 3

Proverbs 27:23-24 Be sure you know the condition of your flocks, give careful attention to your herds; for riches do not endure forever, and a crown is not secure for all generations.

....
....
....
....
....
....
....
....
....

Week 4

Luke 12:34 For where your treasure is, there your heart will be also.

....
....
....
....
....
....
....

How do these verses apply to your focus word for this year?

....
....
....
....
....
....

Hebrews 13:5 Keep your lives free from the love of money and be content with what you have, because God has said, "Never will I leave you; never will I forsake you."

My Focus This Week:
....
....
....
....

My Affirmation or Focus Statement:
....
....
....
....

Sunday:

AM	PM
My prayer for today	Where I saw/heard God
What I'm giving to God	Successes
Distractions to be aware of	Challenges
I'm grateful for	Prayer requests

Monday: AM / PM

AM	PM
My prayer for today	Where I saw/heard God
What I'm giving to God	Successes
Distractions to be aware of	Challenges
I'm grateful for	Prayer requests

Tuesday: AM / PM

AM	PM
My prayer for today	Where I saw/heard God
What I'm giving to God	Successes
Distractions to be aware of	Challenges
I'm grateful for	Prayer requests

Wednesday: AM   PM

My prayer for today	Where I saw/heard God
What I'm giving to God	Successes
Distractions to be aware of	Challenges
I'm grateful for	Prayer requests

Thursday: AM   PM

My prayer for today	Where I saw/heard God
What I'm giving to God	Successes
Distractions to be aware of	Challenges
I'm grateful for	Prayer requests

Friday: AM   PM

My prayer for today	Where I saw/heard God
What I'm giving to God	Successes
Distractions to be aware of	Challenges
I'm grateful for	Prayer requests

Saturday: AM   PM

My prayer for today	Where I saw/heard God
What I'm giving to God	Successes
Distractions to be aware of	Challenges
I'm grateful for	Prayer requests

Week Two

Proverbs 21:5 The plans of the diligent lead to profit as surely as haste leads to poverty.

My Focus This Week:
....
....
....
....

My Affirmation or Focus Statement:
....
....
....
....

Sunday:

AM	PM
My prayer for today	Where I saw/heard God
What I'm giving to God	Successes
Distractions to be aware of	Challenges
I'm grateful for	Prayer requests

Monday: AM   PM

AM	PM
My prayer for today	Where I saw/heard God
What I'm giving to God	Successes
Distractions to be aware of	Challenges
I'm grateful for	Prayer requests

Tuesday: AM   PM

AM	PM
My prayer for today	Where I saw/heard God
What I'm giving to God	Successes
Distractions to be aware of	Challenges
I'm grateful for	Prayer requests

Wednesday: AM   PM

My prayer for today	Where I saw/heard God
What I'm giving to God	Successes
Distractions to be aware of	Challenges
I'm grateful for	Prayer requests

Thursday: AM   PM

My prayer for today	Where I saw/heard God
What I'm giving to God	Successes
Distractions to be aware of	Challenges
I'm grateful for	Prayer requests

Friday: AM   PM

My prayer for today	Where I saw/heard God
What I'm giving to God	Successes
Distractions to be aware of	Challenges
I'm grateful for	Prayer requests

Saturday: AM   PM

My prayer for today	Where I saw/heard God
What I'm giving to God	Successes
Distractions to be aware of	Challenges
I'm grateful for	Prayer requests

Proverbs 27:23-24 Be sure you know the condition of your flocks, give careful attention to your herds; for riches do not endure forever, and a crown is not secure for all generations.

My Focus This Week:
....
....
....
....

My Affirmation or Focus Statement:
....
....
....
....

Sunday: AM | PM

My prayer for today	Where I saw/heard God
What I'm giving to God	Successes
Distractions to be aware of	Challenges
I'm grateful for	Prayer requests

Wednesday: AM   PM

My prayer for today	Where I saw/heard God
What I'm giving to God	Successes
Distractions to be aware of	Challenges
I'm grateful for	Prayer requests

Thursday: AM   PM

My prayer for today	Where I saw/heard God
What I'm giving to God	Successes
Distractions to be aware of	Challenges
I'm grateful for	Prayer requests

Friday: AM | PM

My prayer for today	Where I saw/heard God
What I'm giving to God	Successes
Distractions to be aware of	Challenges
I'm grateful for	Prayer requests

Saturday: AM | PM

My prayer for today	Where I saw/heard God
What I'm giving to God	Successes
Distractions to be aware of	Challenges
I'm grateful for	Prayer requests

Luke 12:34 For where your treasure is, there your heart will be also.

My Focus This Week:

....
....
....
....

My Affirmation or Focus Statement:

....
....
....
....

Sunday:

AM	PM
My prayer for today	Where I saw/heard God
What I'm giving to God	Successes
Distractions to be aware of	Challenges
I'm grateful for	Prayer requests

Monday: AM   PM

My prayer for today	Where I saw/heard God
What I'm giving to God	Successes
Distractions to be aware of	Challenges
I'm grateful for	Prayer requests

Tuesday: AM   PM

My prayer for today	Where I saw/heard God
What I'm giving to God	Successes
Distractions to be aware of	Challenges
I'm grateful for	Prayer requests

Wednesday: AMPM

My prayer for today	Where I saw/heard God
What I'm giving to God	Successes
Distractions to be aware of	Challenges
I'm grateful for	Prayer requests

Thursday: AMPM

My prayer for today	Where I saw/heard God
What I'm giving to God	Successes
Distractions to be aware of	Challenges
I'm grateful for	Prayer requests

Friday: AM   PM

My prayer for today	Where I saw/heard God
What I'm giving to God	Successes
Distractions to be aware of	Challenges
I'm grateful for	Prayer requests

Saturday: AM   PM

My prayer for today	Where I saw/heard God
What I'm giving to God	Successes
Distractions to be aware of	Challenges
I'm grateful for	Prayer requests

Monthly Reflection

Use this space to reflect on your previous month.

....
....
....
....
....
....
....
....
....
....
....
....
....
....
....
....
....
....
....
....
....
....
....
....
....

Month Eleven: Margin

"I am only one person. I have one brain, one heart, two hands, and two feet. I must set limits and boundaries within my means. Saying yes to one thing means saying no to something else. God did not create me to do it all."

These are words I say to myself every day. Not always in that order, and not always all of them. But if I don't remind myself of these things, I will let my tendency to overcommit take over my life, and I will mourn all the lost free time, family time, and fun time.

When you leave blanks in your calendar, you're giving God an opportunity to fill those spaces. Even if boredom fills that space, that's okay. Some of the greatest ideas were born out of boredom!

When my kids were little, I used to host our playgroup's annual Easter egg hunt. One year, I just couldn't do it. I don't remember why, but I couldn't. I stressed that if I didn't do it, it wouldn't happen, or if it did, it wouldn't be as good as if I did it. I listened to God, and passed it on. The mom who took it over ROCKED it, and I actually enjoyed myself during the event because I wasn't trying to make sure everything was going perfectly.

It was a tough lesson to learn, and there's always a chance if you stop doing something you always do, that will be the end of it. Our Girl Scout experience ended after four years when I resigned as co-leader. My girl only liked the friends and the field trips, and I was working about twenty hours a week on obligatory troop stuff the girls didn't really care about. None of the other moms could fill my role, so we took all the cookie money we'd earned and spent the night at a cabin at Disney's Fort Wilderness. It was unforgettable, hard-earned, and a beautiful closing activity to four years of scouting.

Do you overbook yourself? Or is your calendar empty? Either way, go back to your focus word and your goals. If an activity isn't serving you or supporting your goals or a long-term vision, cut it. If you have room to add something that supports, seek out opportunities to grow. Jot down a few ideas for evenings out your calendar and choosing intentional activities. (extra pages in back)

....
....
....
....

Verses for the Month

Write these verses by hand at the beginning of each week. Then record any thoughts, feelings, or reflections that come to mind.

Week 1
Jonah 2:8 Those who cling to worthless idols turn away from God's love for them.

....
....
....
....
....
....
....
....
....

Week 2
Mark 6:33 But many who saw them leaving recognized them and ran on foot from all the towns and got there ahead of them.

....
....
....
....
....
....
....
....
....
....

Week 3

Romans 12:2 Do not conform to the pattern of this world, but be transformed by the renewing of your mind. Then you will be able to test and approve what God's will is—His good, pleasing and perfect will.

....
....
....
....
....
....
....
....
....

Week 4

Proverbs 21:5 The plans of the diligent lead to profit as surely as haste leads to poverty.

....
....
....
....
....
....
....

How do these verses apply to your focus word for this year?

....
....
....
....
....
....

Jonah 2:8 Those who cling to worthless idols turn away from God's love for them.

My Focus This Week:
....
....
....
....

My Affirmation or Focus Statement:
....
....
....
....

Sunday:

AM	PM
My prayer for today	Where I saw/heard God
What I'm giving to God	Successes
Distractions to be aware of	Challenges
I'm grateful for	Prayer requests

Monday: AM   PM

My prayer for today	Where I saw/heard God
What I'm giving to God	Successes
Distractions to be aware of	Challenges
I'm grateful for	Prayer requests

Tuesday: AM   PM

My prayer for today	Where I saw/heard God
What I'm giving to God	Successes
Distractions to be aware of	Challenges
I'm grateful for	Prayer requests

Wednesday: AM   PM

AM	PM
My prayer for today	Where I saw/heard God
What I'm giving to God	Successes
Distractions to be aware of	Challenges
I'm grateful for	Prayer requests

Thursday: AM   PM

AM	PM
My prayer for today	Where I saw/heard God
What I'm giving to God	Successes
Distractions to be aware of	Challenges
I'm grateful for	Prayer requests

Friday: AM   PM

My prayer for today	Where I saw/heard God
What I'm giving to God	Successes
Distractions to be aware of	Challenges
I'm grateful for	Prayer requests

Saturday: AM   PM

My prayer for today	Where I saw/heard God
What I'm giving to God	Successes
Distractions to be aware of	Challenges
I'm grateful for	Prayer requests

Mark 6:33 But many who saw them leaving recognized them and ran on foot from all the towns and got there ahead of them.

My Focus This Week:
....
....
....
....

My Affirmation or Focus Statement:
....
....
....
....

Sunday:

AM	PM
My prayer for today	Where I saw/heard God
What I'm giving to God	Successes
Distractions to be aware of	Challenges
I'm grateful for	Prayer requests

Monday: AM   PM

My prayer for today	Where I saw/heard God
What I'm giving to God	Successes
Distractions to be aware of	Challenges
I'm grateful for	Prayer requests

Tuesday: AM   PM

My prayer for today	Where I saw/heard God
What I'm giving to God	Successes
Distractions to be aware of	Challenges
I'm grateful for	Prayer requests

Wednesday: AM — PM

My prayer for today	Where I saw/heard God
What I'm giving to God	Successes
Distractions to be aware of	Challenges
I'm grateful for	Prayer requests

Thursday: AM — PM

My prayer for today	Where I saw/heard God
What I'm giving to God	Successes
Distractions to be aware of	Challenges
I'm grateful for	Prayer requests

Friday: AM   PM

My prayer for today	Where I saw/heard God
What I'm giving to God	Successes
Distractions to be aware of	Challenges
I'm grateful for	Prayer requests

Saturday: AM   PM

My prayer for today	Where I saw/heard God
What I'm giving to God	Successes
Distractions to be aware of	Challenges
I'm grateful for	Prayer requests

Romans 12:2 Do not conform to the pattern of this world, but be transformed by the renewing of your mind. Then you will be able to test and approve what God's will is—His good, pleasing and perfect will.

My Focus This Week:
....
....
....
....

My Affirmation or Focus Statement:
....
....
....
....

Sunday:

AM	PM
My prayer for today	Where I saw/heard God
What I'm giving to God	Successes
Distractions to be aware of	Challenges
I'm grateful for	Prayer requests

Monday: AM   PM

My prayer for today	Where I saw/heard God
What I'm giving to God	Successes
Distractions to be aware of	Challenges
I'm grateful for	Prayer requests

Tuesday: AM   PM

My prayer for today	Where I saw/heard God
What I'm giving to God	Successes
Distractions to be aware of	Challenges
I'm grateful for	Prayer requests

Wednesday: AM   PM

My prayer for today	Where I saw/heard God
What I'm giving to God	Successes
Distractions to be aware of	Challenges
I'm grateful for	Prayer requests

Thursday: AM   PM

My prayer for today	Where I saw/heard God
What I'm giving to God	Successes
Distractions to be aware of	Challenges
I'm grateful for	Prayer requests

Friday: AM   PM

My prayer for today	Where I saw/heard God
What I'm giving to God	Successes
Distractions to be aware of	Challenges
I'm grateful for	Prayer requests

Saturday: AM   PM

My prayer for today	Where I saw/heard God
What I'm giving to God	Successes
Distractions to be aware of	Challenges
I'm grateful for	Prayer requests

Proverbs 21:5 The plans of the diligent lead to profit as surely as haste leads to poverty.

My Focus This Week:

....
....
....
....

My Affirmation or Focus Statement:

....
....
....
....

Sunday: AM   PM

My prayer for today	Where I saw/heard God
What I'm giving to God	Successes
Distractions to be aware of	Challenges
I'm grateful for	Prayer requests

Monday: AM   PM

My prayer for today	Where I saw/heard God
What I'm giving to God	Successes
Distractions to be aware of	Challenges
I'm grateful for	Prayer requests

Tuesday: AM   PM

My prayer for today	Where I saw/heard God
What I'm giving to God	Successes
Distractions to be aware of	Challenges
I'm grateful for	Prayer requests

Wednesday: AM · PM

My prayer for today	Where I saw/heard God

What I'm giving to God	Successes

Distractions to be aware of	Challenges

I'm grateful for	Prayer requests

Thursday: AM · PM

My prayer for today	Where I saw/heard God

What I'm giving to God	Successes

Distractions to be aware of	Challenges

I'm grateful for	Prayer requests

Friday: AM PM

My prayer for today	Where I saw/heard God
What I'm giving to God	Successes
Distractions to be aware of	Challenges
I'm grateful for	Prayer requests

Saturday: AM PM

My prayer for today	Where I saw/heard God
What I'm giving to God	Successes
Distractions to be aware of	Challenges
I'm grateful for	Prayer requests

Monthly Reflection

Use this space to reflect on your previous month.

....
....
....
....
....
....
....
....
....
....
....
....
....
....
....
....
....
....
....
....
....
....
....
....
....

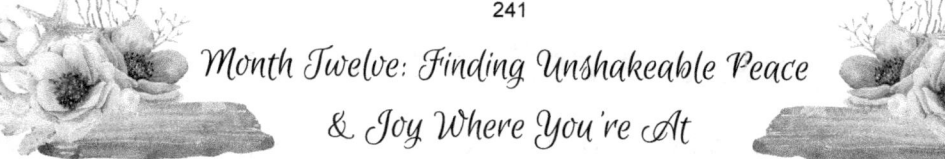

Month Twelve: Finding Unshakeable Peace & Joy Where You're At

You know the sun is still shining behind the cloudiest sky. In the same way, God is ever-present, even when you can't see or feel Him. Trusting He's there and knowing He wants the best for me is sometimes a test of faith. But the cost of losing faith is hopelessness. And we all know where hopelessness leads.

You can learn to catch yourself before you spiral down what I call the Hopeless Hole, the route that will take you to rock bottom; your own personal hell. Since I love alliteration and acronyms (thinking them up is one of my strengths), I devised this little trick to help me regain control when I feel unbalanced or overcome by big emotions.

SIRE, because, God is our spiritual father. Don't forget it!

First, SIT. Find a place to sit, or kneel, if you prefer. Just get off your feet. Then INHALE deeply, for as many beats as you physically can. As you hold that last breath in place, pray for REST. Then, EXHALE as slowly as possible. Repeat until your heartbeat has regulated and you feel like you can think clearly and realistically.

WE are in control of our emotions. We CHOOSE how to react, except in the case of a visceral reaction. Gut punches like unexpected news or sudden danger are the exception. But if someone does you wrong, if your child spills the milk for the third time in one morning, or you find out your car breaks down on the highway, you can learn to steady yourself and react in a controlled, intentional way.

Sometimes we need more help, and that's okay. There are a lot people and places we can seek out to help guide us spiritually, mentally, and emotionally. If your Hopeless Hole becomes more that you can manage on your own, do please reach out for help.

Do you tend to overreact emotionally? When bad things happen, do you blame God? Write a bit about what you think you need to do to live in peace each day. (extra pages in back)

....
....
....
....

Verses for the Month

Write these verses by hand at the beginning of each week. Then record any thoughts, feelings or reflections that come to mind.

Week 1
Psalm 17:6 I call on you, my God, for you will answer me; turn your ear to me and hear my prayer.

....
....
....
....
....
....
....
....
....

Week 2
Matthew 18:20 For where two or three gather in my name, there am I with them.

....
....
....
....
....
....
....
....
....

Week 3

2 Corinthians 9:8 And God is able to bless you abundantly, so that in all things at all times, having all that you need, you will abound in every good work.

....
....
....
....
....
....
....
....
....

Week 4

John 5:15 The man went away and told the Jewish leaders that it was Jesus who had made him well.

....
....
....
....
....
....
....

How do these verses apply to your focus word for this year?

....
....
....
....
....

Psalm 17:6 I call on you, my God, for you will answer me; turn your ear to me and hear my prayer.

My Focus This Week:
....
....
....
....

My Affirmation or Focus Statement:
....
....
....
....

Sunday:

AM	PM
My prayer for today	Where I saw/heard God
What I'm giving to God	Successes
Distractions to be aware of	Challenges
I'm grateful for	Prayer requests

Monday: AM   PM

My prayer for today	Where I saw/heard God
What I'm giving to God	Successes
Distractions to be aware of	Challenges
I'm grateful for	Prayer requests

Tuesday: AM   PM

My prayer for today	Where I saw/heard God
What I'm giving to God	Successes
Distractions to be aware of	Challenges
I'm grateful for	Prayer requests

Wednesday: AM   PM

My prayer for today	Where I saw/heard God
What I'm giving to God	Successes
Distractions to be aware of	Challenges
I'm grateful for	Prayer requests

Thursday: AM   PM

My prayer for today	Where I saw/heard God
What I'm giving to God	Successes
Distractions to be aware of	Challenges
I'm grateful for	Prayer requests

Friday:　　AM　　　　　　　　　　　PM

My prayer for today	Where I saw/heard God
What I'm giving to God	Successes
Distractions to be aware of	Challenges
I'm grateful for	Prayer requests

Saturday:　　AM　　　　　　　　　　　PM

My prayer for today	Where I saw/heard God
What I'm giving to God	Successes
Distractions to be aware of	Challenges
I'm grateful for	Prayer requests

Matt 18:20 For where two or three gather in my name, there am I with them.

My Focus This Week:
....
....
....
....

My Affirmation or Focus Statement:
....
....
....
....

Sunday:

AM	PM
My prayer for today	Where I saw/heard God
What I'm giving to God	Successes
Distractions to be aware of	Challenges
I'm grateful for	Prayer requests

Monday: AM / PM

My prayer for today	Where I saw/heard God
What I'm giving to God	Successes
Distractions to be aware of	Challenges
I'm grateful for	Prayer requests

Tuesday: AM / PM

My prayer for today	Where I saw/heard God
What I'm giving to God	Successes
Distractions to be aware of	Challenges
I'm grateful for	Prayer requests

Wednesday: AM   PM

AM	PM
My prayer for today	Where I saw/heard God
What I'm giving to God	Successes
Distractions to be aware of	Challenges
I'm grateful for	Prayer requests

Thursday: AM   PM

AM	PM
My prayer for today	Where I saw/heard God
What I'm giving to God	Successes
Distractions to be aware of	Challenges
I'm grateful for	Prayer requests

Friday: AM   PM

My prayer for today	Where I saw/heard God
What I'm giving to God	Successes
Distractions to be aware of	Challenges
I'm grateful for	Prayer requests

Saturday: AM   PM

My prayer for today	Where I saw/heard God
What I'm giving to God	Successes
Distractions to be aware of	Challenges
I'm grateful for	Prayer requests

2 Corinthians 9:8 And God is able to bless you abundantly, so that in all things at all times, having all that you need, you will abound in every good work.

My Focus This Week:
....
....
....
....

My Affirmation or Focus Statement:
....
....
....
....

Sunday:

AM	PM
My prayer for today	Where I saw/heard God
What I'm giving to God	Successes
Distractions to be aware of	Challenges
I'm grateful for	Prayer requests

Monday: AM   PM

My prayer for today	Where I saw/heard God
What I'm giving to God	Successes
Distractions to be aware of	Challenges
I'm grateful for	Prayer requests

Tuesday: AM   PM

My prayer for today	Where I saw/heard God
What I'm giving to God	Successes
Distractions to be aware of	Challenges
I'm grateful for	Prayer requests

Wednesday: AM — PM

My prayer for today	Where I saw/heard God

What I'm giving to God	Successes

Distractions to be aware of	Challenges

I'm grateful for	Prayer requests

Thursday: AM — PM

My prayer for today	Where I saw/heard God

What I'm giving to God	Successes

Distractions to be aware of	Challenges

I'm grateful for	Prayer requests

Friday: AM   PM

My prayer for today	Where I saw/heard God
What I'm giving to God	Successes
Distractions to be aware of	Challenges
I'm grateful for	Prayer requests

Saturday: AM   PM

My prayer for today	Where I saw/heard God
What I'm giving to God	Successes
Distractions to be aware of	Challenges
I'm grateful for	Prayer requests

John 5:15 The man went away and told the Jewish leaders that it was Jesus who had made him well.

My Focus This Week:

....
....
....
....

My Affirmation or Focus Statement:

....
....
....
....

Sunday:

AM	PM
My prayer for today	Where I saw/heard God
What I'm giving to God	Successes
Distractions to be aware of	Challenges
I'm grateful for	Prayer requests

Monday: AM — PM

My prayer for today	Where I saw/heard God
What I'm giving to God	Successes
Distractions to be aware of	Challenges
I'm grateful for	Prayer requests

Tuesday: AM — PM

My prayer for today	Where I saw/heard God
What I'm giving to God	Successes
Distractions to be aware of	Challenges
I'm grateful for	Prayer requests

Wednesday: AM PM

My prayer for today	Where I saw/heard God
What I'm giving to God	Successes
Distractions to be aware of	Challenges
I'm grateful for	Prayer requests

Thursday: AM PM

My prayer for today	Where I saw/heard God
What I'm giving to God	Successes
Distractions to be aware of	Challenges
I'm grateful for	Prayer requests

Friday: AM   PM

My prayer for today	Where I saw/heard God
What I'm giving to God	Successes
Distractions to be aware of	Challenges
I'm grateful for	Prayer requests

Saturday: AM   PM

My prayer for today	Where I saw/heard God
What I'm giving to God	Successes
Distractions to be aware of	Challenges
I'm grateful for	Prayer requests

Monthly Reflection

Use this space to reflect on your previous month.

....
....
....
....
....
....
....
....
....
....
....
....
....
....
....
....
....
....
....
....
....
....
....
....
....
....

Quarterly Reflection

***Proverbs 22:7* The rich rule over the poor, and the borrower is slave to the lender.**

This doesn't only apply to finances. Reflect on this and how it relates to your life and experiences.

Answered Prayers

What prayers did God answer this quarter?

RECAP: FAITH AND YOUR SPIRIT

You may have noticed there wasn't any one month dedicated to your faith or spirituality. I hope you've come to realize that it is not a separate topic, rather, it is intended to be weaved into and influence everything else. Fill out the Faith Inventory again and compare it to the one you completed in the beginning.

Date: ....

	Always	Sometimes	Never
I purposefully set aside time daily to be with God			
I feel connected to God			
I can hear God			
I listen to God			
I give my day to God			
I have peace things will work out			
I am productive, but not busy			
I give myself grace			
I give others grace			
I am able to keep calm in stressful situations			
I am able to rest			
My body feels loose and light			
I can express gratitude where I am			
I am a peace with my past			
I can find joy in everywhere			
I am content and at rest			
My faith is unshakable			

Do you feel like you've made gains? If not, look back over your progress and determine areas to devote additional time so that you may reach your goals.

Reflect on what you've accomplished over the past twelve months:

....
....
....
....
....
....
....
....
....
....
....
....
....
....
....
....
....
....
....
....
....
....
....
....
....
....
....

Next Steps

Meditate on these verses and reflect on how your mindset has grown since you started this book. Journal about the work still ahead, and what you want to focus on over the next twelve months.

Psalm 46:10 He says, "Be still, and know that I am God; I will be exalted among the nations, I will be exalted in the earth."

....
....
....
....
....
....
....
....
....

James 1:2-4 Consider it pure joy, my brothers and sisters, whenever you face trials of many kinds, because you know that the testing of your faith produces perseverance. Let perseverance finish its work so that you may be mature and complete, not lacking anything.

....
....
....
....
....
....
....
....

Psalm 145:18-19 The LORD is near to all who call on Him, to all who call on Him in truth. He fulfills the desires of those who fear Him; He hears their cry and saves them.

....
....
....
....
....
....
....
....

Romans 12:12 Be joyful in hope, patient in affliction, faithful in prayer.

....
....
....
....
....
....
....
....

Thoughts for next year:
....
....
....
....
....
....
....

About the Author

Kerry Evelyn is an author, instructor, and writing judge in the Orlando literary community, mentoring student writers and teaching classes for Writer's Atelier, libraries, and professional organizations. Her sweet romance novels feature small towns, a touch of the supernatural, and charming characters pursuing happily-every-afters. Fueled on faith, Dunkin' iced coffee, and a love for people, including her amazing family, Kerry loves (in ever-changing order) books, boybands, cats, hockey, sweet drinks, taking selfies, traveling, and the madness of getting the stories in her head onto the page. Find out more and sign up for her newsletter by scanning the QR code or visiting KerryEvelyn.com.

Acknowledgements

I'm incredibly grateful to everyone who has inspired me on my faith journey: My family, church friends and mentors, Club Mommers, Goalmates, MMU'ers, Fierce BAIJNS, Boom Sisters, Write from His Hearties, CCS moms, Legacy Ladies, and Crane's Cove VIPs...you are all part of my story. God bless you.

Also by Kerry Evelyn

The Crane's Cove Series
Love on the Edge
Love on the Rocks
Love on the Beach
Love on the Fly

Crane's Cove Short Stories
A Night at the Inn: A Lizzie Borden Short Story
The Cotton Candy Caper: A Fall Carnival Story
A Night in the Passage: A Crane's Cove Short Story
The Fisherman Nutcracker: A Whimsical Christmas Story
A Night in the Cabin: A Crane's Cove Short Story
A Second Shot at Love

Palmer City Voltage Hockey Romance
Love on the Ice
Cruising on Ice
Christmas on Ice

Cat's Paw Cove Books
Moon Mist Manor Book 1: Christmas at Moon Mist Manor
Moon Mist Manor Book 2: Love Overrules the Lawyer
Moon Mist Manor Book 3: The Beachcomber's Buccaneer Bounty

Other Stories by Kerry Evelyn
City Nights (How I Met My Other Anthology)
Fenway: A Beacon of Hope (How I Met My Other 2)
Bird's Eye View (Once Upon Academy)
Phoenix Rising (Once Upon Academy)

More Focus Journals

All Available on Amazon!

Teachers' Journal for Balance
ISBN: 978-1949935165

From Burnout to Balance: A Nursing Resilience Journal
ISBN: 978-1949935240

Quarantine Journal for Sanity
ISBN: 978-1949935189

Creatives' Journal for Inspiration and Productivity
ISBN: 978-1949935196

Mothers' Journal for Inner Peace
ISBN: 978-1949935172

More From Orange Blossom Publishing

Mass by Kristin Durfee
How do you choose between your faith and your future?

Sixteen-year-old Stevie Albie is a religious person, but nothing prepares her for meeting Mary. Like *the* Mary, mother of Jesus. Just as Stevie becomes convinced she has a special connection with God, doctors discover a brain tumor in her frontal lobe they claim is causing the hallucinations.

Her parents insist on removing the tumor as quickly as possible, but Stevie isn't so sure. Feeling special for the first time in her life, she runs away to a religious cult that's convinced her visions are their salvation and vow to protect her. But as time goes on she suspects they have their own agenda. Torn on who to trust, Stevie wonders if she'll have to choose: her visions or her future?

Available on Amazon, Barnes & Noble, WalMart, and Target

Visit www.orangeblossombooks.com for more!